Shirley

Treasury of Appliqué Quilt Patterns

Maggie Malone

Sterling Publishing Co., Inc. New York

Library of Congress Cataloging-in-Publication Data

Malone, Maggie, 1942–
    Treasury of appliqué quilt patterns / by Maggie Malone.
        p.   cm.
    Includes index.
    ISBN 0-8069-0746-0
    1. Appliqué—Patterns.   2. Quilting—Patterns.   I. Title.
TT779.M28   1995
746.46—dc20   95-40526
                                                              CIP

Front jacket photograph by Nancy Palubniak

Edited by Isabel Stein, with assistance from Cassandra Thoreson of the Brooklyn
Quilters' Guild, Brooklyn, New York

10   9   8   7   6   5   4   3   2   1

Published by Sterling Publishing Company, Inc.
387 Park Avenue South, New York, N.Y. 10016
© 1996 by Maggie Malone
Distributed in Canada by Sterling Publishing
% Canadian Manda Group, One Atlantic Avenue, Suite 105
Toronto, Ontario, Canada M6K 3E7
Distributed in Great Britain and Europe by Cassell PLC
Wellington House, 125 Strand, London WC2R OBB, England
Distributed in Australia by Capricorn Link (Australia) Pty Ltd.
P.O. Box 6651, Baulkham Hills, Business Centre, NSW 2153, Australia
Printed and bound in Hong Kong

Sterling ISBN 0-8069-0746-0

CONTENTS

PREFACE

Over the years, my quiltmaking efforts have been focused on geometric patchwork designs. The play of color and pattern offered endless possibilities for design variation.

While I had seen truly breathtaking traditional appliqué quilts, whenever I had tried to execute one I had found the techniques too stilted and boring to hold my interest for long. Preparing this book has been a journey of discovery. The creativity I found among the appliqué quilters who allowed me to photograph their quilts has changed my viewpoint forever. Appliqué can truly be an art form, a painting done with thread and fabric, but you needn't be an artist to create a stunning appliqué quilt. The traditional patterns presented in this book are a good starting point, but don't stop there! Everything under the sun and beyond can be successfully interpreted in appliqué.

This book has been designed for the beginner as well as the experienced quiltmaker. Basic instructions will give you a good start if you are new to appliqué. Some of the techniques presented may be new to the experienced quilter, or may merely serve as a refresher. I have provided full-size appliqué patterns for over 70 traditional block designs. Color photographs of the blocks are also included to serve as a guideline to placement and for color suggestions. You will find old familiar favorites as well as some more unusual designs.

There are also many full-color photographs of completed quilts in the "Quiltmakers' Gallery" section of the book. Many of the quilts in the gallery section were made from designs that were lovingly passed from friend to friend; some are from kits or pattern books; some appeared in newspapers or other sources; some were original creations of the quilter. We have made every effort to credit the original creators of the patterns, as well as the quilters, in the permissions and photo credits section.

Most of the quilters whose work is pictured in the Quiltmakers' Gallery have had no formal art training, yet they have created truly stunning quilts. When I was talking with Peggy Deierhoi, one of the quilters featured, she asked me if I considered these quilts to be art quilts. I had to say "no." Art quilts are designed to be hung in galleries, to be admired from afar. The quilts shown here, with the exception of those quilts by Clare Murray and Nancy Watts, were made to be used and enjoyed. They invite you to admire their design and workmanship, but they also invite you to wrap up in them on a cold winter night. These are provided to show the endless possibilities of appliqué and to serve as inspiration as you travel along the road of your own development as a quilter.

Maggie Malone

Copley, Ohio

Royal Cross, appliquéd and quilted by Anne Doherty, 1990. Design by Judie Rothermel, Schoolhouse Designs.

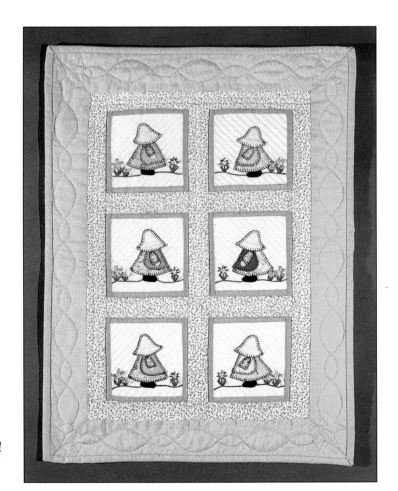

Miniature Sunbonnet Sue was appliquéd and quilted by Leita E. Shahan in 1994 from a traditional design.

Appliqué Basics

Appliqué is the simple technique of sewing a fabric cutout onto a larger piece of fabric, or background block. The major difficulty encountered is in learning to turn under the seam allowances of the appliqué pieces smoothly. In the following pages you will find several techniques that will make this task a little easier. Select one or a combination of techniques, or make up your own. There is no right or wrong way to do appliqué. Choose the most comfortable method for you that achieves the results you want with the least amount of hassle. Quilting is supposed to be a fun and enjoyable pastime.

CHOOSING AND PREPARING FABRIC

As with all quilting, the best choice is 100% cotton. It is soft and pliable and forms a sharp crease when the seam allowances are pressed under. I would also recommend a 65%/35% cotton–polyester blend. The high cotton content makes the fabric more pliable, but you also get the advantage of the colorfastness and durability of polyester. I know I sound like a heretic when I recommend polyester, but it has been my experience that 100% cotton does not hold up well to frequent washing. You will begin to see wear within three or four washings. Avoid a higher polyester percentage in the fabric. The more polyester, the harder the fabric is to work with, and it will not hold a crease. Also avoid percale (the fabric many sheets are made of) because it is so closely woven that it is very difficult to quilt through.

All fabrics used should be washed, dried and ironed before cutting, as they shrink in washing, especially the first washing. Test each fabric for colorfastness by swishing a small piece of it around in warm soapy wa-

ter. If a fabric "bleeds" (the color comes out in the water), do not use it in your quilt. Trim off the selvages and discard them, as they are difficult to quilt through.

HAND APPLIQUÉ OR MACHINE APPLIQUÉ?

Traditionally, appliqué was done by hand and was frequently used for very formal, elegant quilts. I think hand appliqué is the best choice, although there are some machine techniques that can be almost as invisible as hand appliqué. If you find the process of sewing to be a very enjoyable part of quiltmaking and you don't become frustrated at the slow pace, hand appliqué is for you. Interesting textures can be achieved by hand appliqué using crochet cotton or lightweight yarn and a blanket stitch or other decorative hand stitch to appliqué some of the simpler patterns.

Before you start cutting out your appliqués, you need to decide how you're going to attach them. This will affect whether you need to cut them with a seam allowance or not. If you never have tried appliqué before, make up a sample block using each method described, to see which you prefer. Many of the fine quilts you see in the "Quiltmakers' Gallery" section of the book were done by hand appliqué. An experienced quilter can make almost invisible stitches by hand appliqué; however, hand appliqué takes longer than machine appliqué. Some of the quilts in the gallery section took years to complete. Machine appliqué has the advantage of being faster to do and stronger. For a quilt that is going to be washed frequently, or if you need to finish a project quickly, machine appliqué might be for you. Decorative stitches such as satin stitch can be done by machine appliqué.

Machine Appliqué Overview

In machine appliqué, the pieces are sewn on the background by machine. Machine appliqué using a satin stitch or a hem stitch adds a homey touch to casual designs like the sunbonnet patterns. Floral designs with large, simple pieces also look good with machine appliqué. There are several methods of machine appliqué. You could cut the appliqués with no seam allowances, fuse them to the background fabric with fusible webbing, and satin stitch the pieces in place. Another machine appliqué possibility is to cut the appliqués *with* seam allowances, turn the seam allowances under, and machine blindstitch the appliqué pieces in place with colorless nylon monofilament, or using a decorative stitch with contrasting color of thread. Machine appliqué will be discussed in more detail later on. You will need a sewing machine that can sew zigzag stitches to do machine satin stitch, and one that can do machine blindstitch, if you want to attach the appliqués that way.

Hand Appliqué Overview

If you are doing hand appliqué, you will need to add seam allowances around the templates in this book before you cut out your pieces. One-quarter to one-eighth inch seem allowances are commonly used. If you're just learning to appliqué, cut out a few sample appliqué pieces with ¼-inch seam allowances, some with ³⁄₁₆-inch seam allowances, and some with ⅛-inch seam allowances, and try sewing them on a sample block to see which is most comfortable to you. There are several ways to do hand appliqué, which will be discussed in more detail later on. The stitches may be hidden or decorative. It's probably a good idea to cut out pieces for a block just before you're ready to sew them on, rather than cutting out the pieces for all the blocks at once. This keeps the edges from fraying and keeps them from getting lost.

TOOLS AND SUPPLIES

In addition to fabric, you will need the following basic supplies:

- *Template material:* This can be lightweight cardboard such as a writing tablet back or a shirt box. If you use cardboard, you will need to cut several templates of the same shape as time goes by, because with use the cardboard will compress around the edges and the pattern will become smaller. A better choice is lightweight translucent plastic, either plain or ruled in squares. This can be purchased at a quilt shop or fabric store. The plastic does not deteriorate with use, so you only need to cut one template for each shape. You can lay the sheet over the pattern in the book and trace the pattern directly onto the template material without having to make a separate paper tracing.

- *Tracing paper:* If you are using cardboard, you will need tracing paper to transfer the appliqué patterns from the book to the paper.

- *Paper-glue stick:* For gluing traced patterns onto cardboard and other purposes.

- *Pencils and pens:* #2 graphite pencil for tracing patterns onto paper. Some people use them for marking fabric also. A mechanical pencil will help you keep a thin, light line. You might want to try fabric-marking pencils—water-soluble blue pencils for marking light-colored fabrics and silver, yellow, or white pencils for marking dark fabrics. Test all pencils and pens on a scrap of fabric before using them on your project to be sure the markings wash out. If you use a water-soluble fabric-marking pen, be sure not to iron the fabric before washing out the markings; ironing may set the lines permanently. An indelible black pen or marker for inking in patterns on paper is helpful. It should have a dark enough line to show up through a layer of fabric.

- *Ruler:* a 6″ × 24″ plastic, see-through ruler with inch markings (or centimeters if you work in the metric system) is a good choice for measuring and cutting background blocks and borders.

- *Straight pins:* Silk pins are best for pinning appliqués. You could also use small safety pins.

- *Scissors:* Good quality dressmaker's shears for cutting borders and blocks and a smaller pair of pointed scissors for cutting appliqué pieces. General-purpose scissors for cutting patterns and templates are also needed.

- *Iron:* Any lightweight iron will do, but a small travelling iron is ideal for pressing under seam allowances.

- *Sewing machine* with zigzag capabilities for machine appliqué.

- *Sewing machine needles:* For most machine appliqué, a size 14 universal point needle works best.

- *Hand sewing needles:* The smaller the needle, the smaller the stitch, so you could use betweens, sizes 5 to 11, which are generally used for quilting, or the slightly longer sharps (sizes 9 to 12), used for general sewing.

- *Thimble:* For all hand sewing and quilting. Thimbles are available in leather and plastic, in addition to the traditional metal ones.
- *Beeswax:* used to coat the thread so that it doesn't tangle when you do hand sewing.
- *Hand-quilting thread.* For quilting the blocks after you have attached your appliqués, assembled the quilt top, and basted the quilt layers together.
- *Tear-away stabilizer:* For machine appliqué. A layer of thin, nonwoven material, which is placed beneath the background block to insure that the fabric moves easily while you are sewing, doesn't bunch up, and doesn't get pulled into the sewing machine. Tracing paper may be used instead of the commercially available stabilizer.
- *Lightweight fusible webbing:* A lightweight nonwoven material with a coating on both sides that adheres the appliqué piece to the base fabric when it is pressed with a warm iron; this holds the appliqué in place during stitching. Usually used for machine appliqué. Adds some stiffness to the appliqués, which may make them harder to sew through if you're doing hand appliqué, however.
- *Hand-sewing thread, preferably 100% cotton:* For attaching appliqués to the background block in hand appliqué. It is thinner than quilting thread, and so it is harder to see the stitches. Choose a color close to that of each appliqué, or choose a grayed or darker version of the color.
- *Machine sewing thread:* for machine sewing of appliqués or for machine quilting. Could be all-purpose cotton-wrapped polyester or 100% cotton. For decorative machine stitching of appliqués, you might want to use decorative thread instead.

The following supplies are needed for some of the special techniques presented.

- *Graph paper and colored pencils:* for planning quilt designs and calculating sizes and yardages.
- *Freezer paper:* this is ordinary translucent white freezer paper that is coated on one side with polyethylene. Also available in quilt shops is a special freezer paper that has had graph lines printed on it. Freezer paper can be used in several ways. For instance, you can trace a pattern onto the freezer paper and then adhere it to the fabric,

and cut out the appliqués. Freezer-paper templates can be used to hold the turned-under seam allowances before you appliqué a piece in place.

- *Fabric glue stick:* for temporarily adhering appliqués to the background block and for turning under seam allowances before stitching.
- *Spray starch:* Used to hold seam allowances in place for hand appliqué. Makes a very sharp crease when the seam allowances are turned under and pressed. It can get rather messy; the iron should be cleaned frequently when you use spray starch.

The following tools and supplies are nice to have but not essential:

- *Lightbox:* This tool is wonderful if you do a lot of quilting or other types of crafts. It is a box with a translucent top, illuminated from below by fluorescent lights. Good for tracing patterns onto fabric. Place your pattern on top of the box, lay the fabric over the pattern, and trace it onto the fabric. Lightboxes are available at quilt supply shops or art supply stores. The same effect can be achieved by taping the pattern to a window and taping the fabric over the pattern, but it's not nearly as convenient.
- *Bias press strips:* These narrow, metal or heat-resistant plastic strips are a big time- and finger-saver when preparing long, narrow pieces of fabric for appliquéing, such as stems and vines.

HOW TO MAKE A COMPLETE PATTERN

Choose the appliqué pattern you want from the appliqué patterns section of this book. In most cases the patterns in this book, although they are given full-size, are a fraction of the full pattern, as the full pattern is much larger than the book. On the pattern page it indicates what fraction of the full pattern is shown—for example, ⅛, ½, or ¼. A photo of the finished appliqué is also given, so you can see how the fraction relates to the whole design.

How do you get the full pattern to work with? The patterns are symmetrical, which means that the pattern fraction you are given is reflected (mirrored) without change around an imaginary line called the line of symmetry or rotated about a point (see Figure 1 for more about symmetry).

Half Pattern
For a reflected pattern that is given as ½, take a piece

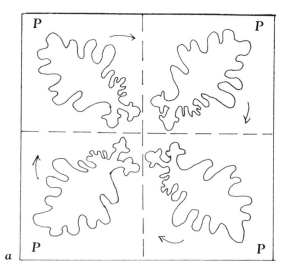

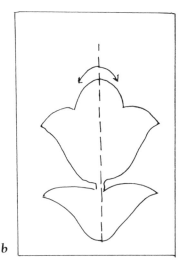

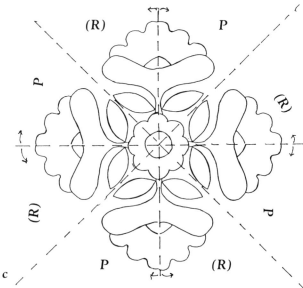

of tracing paper at least as big as your background block will be, fold your tracing paper in half; then trace the pattern in the book, including its center line, in indelible ink onto one half of the piece of tracing paper. Flip the paper over and trace the first half again on the other side of the tracing paper in pencil, aligning the two halves on the center line. Then ink in the drawing of the second half on the front of the tracing paper.

Folded Paper Pattern for Simple ¼ and ⅛ Patterns

For a simple reflected pattern, you can probably avoid tracing the entire pattern by just tracing the fraction and cutting a template from folded paper as follows: Cut a sheet of lightweight tracing paper a few inches bigger than the size of the finished block. For example, assume we are working with a ¼ reflected pattern, like the zinnia pattern (page 100). Fold the tracing paper square into fourths. Open the paper and lay the crease lines along the dashed lines of the pattern in the book, matching the centers of the paper and the design. Trace the pattern onto a quarter section of your paper. Refold the paper. Staple all 4 thicknesses of paper together to keep them from shifting. Cut out the pattern from the paper along the outermost edges of the design, through all 4 thicknesses of paper (Figure 2). Remove the staples and open out your whole pattern template. Use it to trace your main pattern onto the background fabric block.

For a simple ⅛ pattern, you can cut the pattern out on folded tracing paper in the same way as discussed above for the ¼ pattern; just fold your paper on the diagonal after you fold it in quarters to make eight sections. Trace the pattern from the book onto a one-eighth section of your tracing paper, aligning the pattern's dashed lines with the paper's folds. Then refold the paper, staple it through all eight layers to hold it, and cut around the outermost lines of the pattern through all 8 thicknesses at once. When you remove the staples and open the paper out, you will have a template of the complete pattern (although it won't have all the inner lines drawn in).

1. From partial pattern to block pattern. **a:** Quarter pattern rotated about a point of symmetry. **b:** Half pattern reflected about one line to make the full pattern. **c:** Eighth pattern reflected about 4 lines to make the full pattern. P = pattern; (R) = reversed pattern.

2. Cutting a pattern from folded paper.

Complex Patterns

If a complicated pattern is given as ⅛, use an indelible black pen to trace out the ⅛ pattern (P) from the book onto a piece of tracing paper or template plastic the size of the ⅛ pattern. Then take a square of tracing paper at least as large as your planned appliqué block. Fold the paper into quarters and on the diagonals into eighths. Mark the intersection of the lines (the center of the paper) with a black dot. Take your traced-out ⅛ pattern. Align the ⅛ pattern beneath the large tracing paper so the dashed pattern lines fall on the folds and the centers line up. Trace the entire ⅛ pattern, including the guidelines, onto the large tracing paper with indelible pen. For the section to the right of the ⅛ pattern you just traced, you usually need to reverse the ⅛ pattern. Turn the ⅛ pattern over and align it under the large tracing paper next to the section you just traced. Trace the reversed ⅛ pattern onto the block-size tracing paper. Continue tracing each eighth of the pattern, alternating reversed with unreversed eighths, until you are done (Figure 3). In this book (R) indicates a reversed pattern. P indicates an unreversed pattern.

PREPARING AND MARKING THE BACKGROUND BLOCK

The block size given on the pattern is the *smallest* square on which the pattern will fit. You may want to add

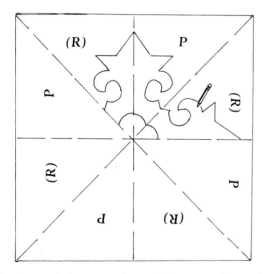

3. *Tracing a whole pattern from a ⅛ pattern. Trace the ⅛ pattern (P) onto a piece of tracing paper the size of ⅛ pattern. Trace the pattern on one-eighth of your large tracing paper. With reversed ⅛ pattern (R) underneath, line up the dashed lines and trace the reversed pattern. Continue tracing eighths, alternating the pattern and reversed pattern until you trace all eight sections.*

more space around the pattern to improve the way it looks, or to make your quilt a certain size. Before you cut all your blocks, do some test sketches of your quilt top with your graph paper or full-size sketches of a block to be sure the block size and design go together well. See the section on Calculating Quilt Size also, before you choose a block size. You can reduce or enlarge a pattern if necessary. In that case, reduce or enlarge your block size by the same percentage you use to change the pattern size.

When cutting your blocks, add at least 1″ or 2″ more than your desired finished block size (without seam allowances) to your block. For a block whose finished size will be 16″, cut an 18″ square, for example. This extra fabric gives you a little leeway to match blocks if they do not line up properly when it comes to assembling the quilt top later on.

Next, fold the block in half top to bottom and press. Open the block out and fold in half from side to side. Press. Open the block and fold on the diagonal in both directions, pressing each fold. Your block is now divided into eighths. The folds are guidelines for placing the appliqués, which may be all that is needed for positioning a simple appliqué pattern.

For a simple pattern, you can mark the pattern onto the background block by tracing around the pattern template, which you have traced and cut out by the folding method (see above). Place the templates on the background fabric block, matching guidelines and block centers, using the photo of the completed block for reference. Trace around the templates, using a fabric marking pencil that shows up well on your fabric or a #2 pencil. Use thin, light lines for this and all fabric marking.

For a complicated pattern with many parts, it's probably better to trace the entire pattern onto your background block. You probably already have made a copy of the whole pattern on tracing paper: If not, trace one as described above in "Complex Patterns." Tape the background block over the complete pattern, aligning the guidelines on the folds in the block. A lightbox comes in handy at this point, or lacking one, tape the fabric and pattern to a window. Use a fabric marking pencil or similar tool and trace the pattern onto the background fabric.

If the design consists of multiple layers of appliqué, such as a flower with a center circle, the bottom appliqué (flower) is the only one you need to mark, because you won't be able to see the center markings once the bottom shape is basted down anyway.

Accuracy in appliqué work is not nearly as important as it is when doing patchwork, but there are exceptions. A few patterns are designed in such a way that they form a continuous design line from block to block. When working with these patterns, it is essential that the design lines meet properly. In this case, it is a good idea to mark the full pattern onto the background block.

CUTTING THE APPLIQUÉ PIECES

Although the block pattern is given in the book on one piece of paper, when you look at the photograph of the appliqué, you see that it is really made up of two or more smaller appliqué patterns. (The exceptions are one-piece patterns such as Fleur de Lis #6.)

Let's assume you've already prepared the background block fabric, as described above. The next step is to make templates of the appliqué pieces. If you have made a copy of your whole pattern, it's easy to trace out each appliqué shape individually, glue it to cardboard, and cut out each appliqué shape from the cardboard for a template. (Plastic template material can be used instead.) Label the front and reversed side of each template. (Some quilters also number each appliqué template and number the pieces correspondingly on their block pattern also.)

The patterns in this book are given without seam allowances. For hand appliqué, you need to add seam allowances around each piece after you trace it. About ¼″ or ³⁄₁₆″ is optimal. Some people add seam allowances for machine appliqué also. The wider the seam allowance, the more likely that you will have to clip it in various places to get it to lie flat.

Because many pieces are little and fray easily, it's a good idea to cut them as you need them. Cut all the pieces you need for a block, but not more. However, you can trace the others onto your appliqué fabrics all at the same time if you wish, leaving space around each for seam allowances. After you have made a block and seen how well your seam allowances worked, you can adjust them when you cut the rest of the pieces.

How you trace and cut your appliqués depends on what method of appliqué you will use, so see the individual sections under "Turning the Seam Allowances and Attaching the Appliqués" for specific details.

Many appliqués are made of layers of fabric stitched on top of each other. For ease of cutting and assembly, it is a good idea to plan the way in which you will cut and sew on the appliqués. Where an appliqué is built up of two more more layers, you can cut the underneath shape as a solid piece of appliqué fabric and cut the top shape from the second fabric to go over it as shown in Figure 4a and b. If you get many layers of

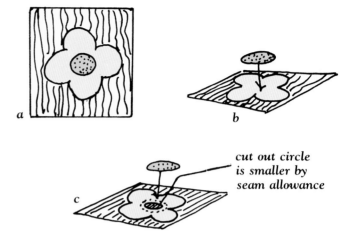

4. *Cutting an appliqué. The finished flower (a) could be cut with a solid underneath shape and a circle of the second fabric superimposed (b); or it could be cut as a flower with a reduced circle cut out and a circle of the second appliqué fabric placed over the cutout (c).*

shapes on top of each other, you can thin them out later from the back of the block by trimming them to reduce bulk, so they won't be hard to quilt through (this is explained later in "Reducing Appliqué Thickness.") Another possibility is to cut the outer (bottom layer) shape from the first appliqué fabric, leaving a space inside for the center shape; then cut the center shape from the second appliqué fabric (see Figure 4c).

To do this, position the center appliqué template on the outer fabric shape and trace around it. Reduce the size of the central shape marked on the outer shape by drawing in a seam allowance on the outer shape, inside the traced central shape, and cut away the reduced central shape from the outer shape's fabric. Trace, cut, prepare, and position the center appliqué over the outer shape, and baste both in place on the block, or otherwise secure it.

General appliqué cutting instructions: Be sure there is enough room around each piece for a seam allowance, if you need one. Trace the appliqué template, using a fabric marking pencil or pen. Move the template far enough to provide for seam allowances and trace again. Repeat for as many appliqués as are needed. If there are any reversed pieces you need to cut, be sure that you flip the template over to the wrong side (reverse it) before tracing them. You don't have to align the template with the straight grain of the fabric, as you do in patchwork. Putting the appliqué on the bias will enable it to stretch and it will be easier to work with.

If you are planning to use a machine satin stitch to sew on the appliqués, it may not be necessary to add seam allowances around the pieces as you cut, because

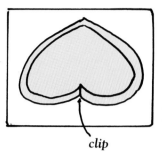

5. *Clipping a seam allowance on an inward point.*

clip

the raw edges of each shape will be protected by the stitches, which are very close together. I personally prefer to add a seam allowance even when doing machine satin stitch, because my machine is an older model that doesn't sew as fine a satin stitch as some of the newer models, there are always stray threads that pop through the satin stitching, and there is a certain amount of fraying as time goes by. Do a test appliqué without seam allowances on your sewing machine to see if the results are good before you cut your project pieces; if they aren't good, add seam allowances to each piece when you cut.

TURNING THE SEAM ALLOWANCES AND ATTACHING THE APPLIQUÉS

The basic goal of all the methods of turning seam allowances is the same: to get the seam allowance to remain turned under the correct amount so you can stitch it in place. For all methods, if an edge of an appliqué piece will be covered by another appliqué piece in the final design, leave the seam allowance unturned on the edge to be covered. You probably will have to clip the seam allowances to make them lie flat when turning a seam allowance on an inward (concave) curve or point; see Figure 5. Clip perpendicular to the seamline, up to a few threads from the seamline. Outside (convex) curves also may need to be clipped at intervals.

Most designs should be sewn down starting from the center pieces, working outwards, but because other pieces may need to be positioned under the central appliqué pieces, it's best to position and baste in place all the pieces for a block before sewing any on permanently. (If you use fusible webbing, you don't need to baste, however; see the section on fusible webbing below.)

The basic method of preparing and attaching appliqués, which our forebears used and many people still do use, is to trace the appliqués onto the right side of their respective appliqué fabrics, add seam allowances, cut out the pieces, and turn the seam allowances over to

the wrong side of each appliqué piece. Seam allowances are clipped as needed, and then each piece is basted in place onto the background block and sewn down by hand appliqué. In the next few pages, several other methods of turning seam allowances and attaching appliqués are described.

Needleturning Method of Hand Appliqué

The seam allowances can be turned under with your needle as you sew. First, trace the appliqué shapes onto the right sides of their respective fabrics, and cut them out, adding seam allowances as you cut. Baste the appliqués into position on the background block, keeping your basting stitches near the center of each piece. Using the middle of the needle (the shank), tuck the seam allowance under the appliqué, making sure you have turned it exactly on the traced seam line. Take a few tiny tacking stitches, then turn under some more of the seam allowance. Start turning the seam allowance under at a place on the appliqué that isn't near a point, if possible. (See the section on Hand Appliqué stitches for more details.)

Freezer Paper on Top Method of Hand Appliqué

One alternative to the basic method of hand appliqué is to trace out the appliqué piece on the unshiny side of freezer paper (the white kind with a polyethylene coating) and cut it out of the paper to use as a template. Then, using a hot iron and no steam, iron and baste the freezer paper template, shiny side down, to the front of the fabric piece from which you will cut the appliqué. Cut the appliqué out of the fabric, adding seam allowances all around (Figure 6a), but leave the template in place as a sewing guide and stabilizer. Then baste the template and appliqué in place on the front of the background block, positioning it correctly by using a lightbox or using the pressed lines as a guide (Figure 6b). Thread your sewing needle with hand sewing thread that has been run through beeswax to keep it from tangling. Using the middle part of the needle, simply turn the seam allowances under as you go, using tacking stitches to hand stitch the appliqué in place (Figure 6c). You may need to clip the seam allowances at the curves in some places. When you're done, snip the basting thread and peel off the freezer paper.

Starch Method of Turning Seam Allowances

This method may be used for machine or hand appliqué. Trace the reversed appliqué shape onto the wrong side of the appliqué fabric, and cut out the appliqué,

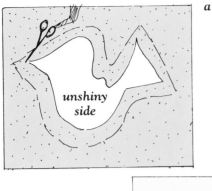

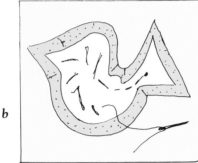

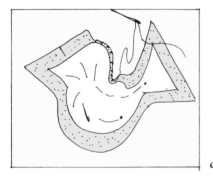

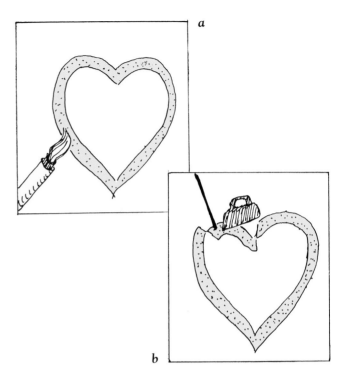

6. *Freezer paper on top method of hand appliqué.* **a:** *Freezer paper pattern piece, shiny side down, is fused to right side of the appliqué fabric. Cut out, adding seam allowances as you go.* **b:** *The cut-out appliqué, with freezer paper still in place, is basted in place on the background block.* **c:** *Seam allowances are needleturned under, using the freezer paper pattern as a guide. Clip seam allowances as necessary.*

7. *Starch method of preparing an appliqué for hand appliqué.* **a:** *Reversed template of pattern is positioned on wrong side of cut-out appliqué; seam allowances are wet with liquid starch.* **b:** *Seam allowances are ironed in place around the template, which is then removed.*

adding a seam allowance as you cut. Take your cardboard template of the appliqué shape and place it face down on the wrong side of the cut-out appliqué piece. Take some liquid starch on a brush or cotton swab, and dab it on the seam allowances (Figure 7a); then iron them down around the template (Figure 7b); clip seam allowances as necessary. Use a toothpick or other stick to hold the seam allowances in place as you iron, to avoid burnt fingers. Remember that you do not need to turn any seam allowance that will lie under another appliqué. After the seam allowances are ironed in place, gently remove the template. Baste the appliqué shape right-side up onto the front of your quilt block

and appliqué it in place, clipping any curves or adjusting any edges, if necessary, to smooth it out.

Fabric Glue Method

Another method of turning seam allowances, one that is particularly useful for simple designs with moderate curves, is to use fabric glue to hold the turned-under seam. Just run the fabric glue stick along the seam allowance and turn the seam allowance over to the wrong side of the appliqué. Baste or fabric-glue the appliqué in place and stitch the appliqué to the background block by hand or by machine appliqué.

Fusible Webbing Method

Fusible webbing is particularly useful for machine appliqué. You can use it to attach appliqués with seam allowances or appliqués without seam allowances. Choose a lightweight webbing so it isn't difficult to sew through. To make appliqués *with seam allowances,* trace the reversed appliqué onto the paper side of the webbing. Cut the shape out of the webbing along the traced lines *without seam allowances.* Fuse the webbing shape to the wrong side of the appliqué fabric (Figure 8a). Cut out the appliqué, adding a seam allowance around the shape as you cut (Figure 8b).

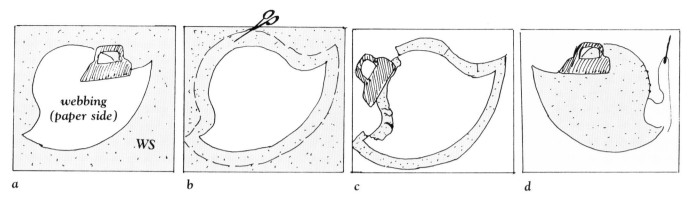

a   *b*   *c*   *d*

8. *Fusible webbing for machine or hand appliqué, with seam allowances.* **a:** *Fuse the cut-out reversed webbing shape on the wrong side of the appliqué fabric.* **b:** *Cut the appliqué out of the fabric, adding seam allowance as you go.* **c:** *Peel the paper off the fusible webbing and tack the seam allowances in place with an iron or fabric glue.* **d:** *Position the appliqué on the background fabric and fuse in place with an iron. Then sew on the appliqué.*

Remove the backing paper from the webbing. Clip the seam allowances of curves at sharp indentations to achieve a smooth turning of the seam allowance. To tack down the seam allowances to the uncovered side of the webbing, use the very tip of the iron and press, following manufacturer's directions, until the seam allowance fabric adheres to the webbing (Figure 8c). If the iron touches the uncovered webbing, the adhesive makes the iron sticky and it will require cleaning. Continue around the appliqué until all seam allowances are adhered to the webbing.

Position the prepared appliqués in the appropriate places on the background block and press it in place, starting with the layers that are closest to the block. The appliqué will stay put without pins, which can distort or shift the piece. The edges are not stuck down, so you can slip other appliqué pieces under the appliqué if need be. If you make a mistake in positioning, the appliqués can be lifted and repositioned with many types of webbing. The webbing becomes a permanent part of the appliqué, but it is light enough to machine quilt through.

To make appliqués *without seam allowances* for machine appliqué using fusible webbing, trace the reversed appliqués onto the paper side of fusible webbing, leaving a little space between each shape, and cut each appliqué out of the webbing with some extra webbing around it. Fuse the webbing piece to the wrong side of your appliqué fabric. Carefully cut the appliqué shape out through the webbing and fabric on the appliqué's outline, without adding any seam allowance. Peel off the paper. Fuse the shape in place on the background block and satin stitch down, using thread that matches each appliqué fabric, changing threads as necessary.

Place a piece of tear-away stabilizer or tracing paper under your block before starting to appliqué, to keep the block from getting pulled into the sewing machine. Work from the center of the block outwards.

Freezer Paper Inside Method of Hand Appliqué
In this method, freezer paper is used to adhere the appliqué piece to the background block. The polyethylene coat of the shiny side of freezer paper temporarily tacks the appliqué in place. You can also baste them in place if you find they tend to fall off. Trace out the *unreversed* appliqué piece on the unshiny side of freezer paper (Figure 9a), without adding seam allowances, and cut out the shape as a template. Place the appliqué fabric wrong-side up and position the reversed freezer paper template on the fabric, shiny side up, and trace around it (Figure 9b). Adding a seam allowance of fabric around the traced shape as you go, cut out the shape from the fabric (Figure 9c). Clip the seam allowances to within a few threads of the seamline at inward curves. Replace the template, shiny side up, on the wrong side of the fabric. Turn the seam allowances over the freezer paper and tack them in place by ironing them onto the freezer paper (Figure 9d), or glue them in place with fabric glue. Then iron the appliqué in place on the background block with a hot iron, shiny paper side down, and appliqué it in place, without removing the freezer paper (Figure 9e). To remove the paper, turn the block over to the back. Cut a slit in the background fabric in the center of the appliqué piece (being careful not to cut through to the front), and pull the freezer paper out through the slit. Use a tweezers if necessary. Close up the slit with hand overcast stitch.

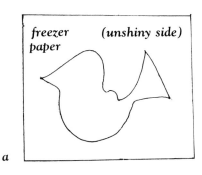

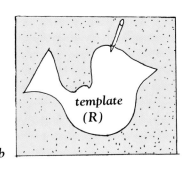

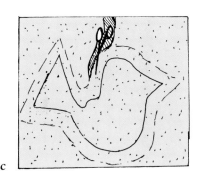

9. *Preparing an appliqué, freezer paper inside method.* **a:** *Trace the appliqué on the unshiny side of freezer paper and cut it out.* **b:** *On the wrong side of the fabric, trace the reversed pattern. Set the paper pattern aside.* **c:** *Cut out the shape from fabric, adding a seam allowance as you go.* **d:** *Replace the paper pattern, shiny side up, on the wrong side of the fabric, and tack the seam allowances in place on the paper with a hot iron.* **e:** *Tack the shape by ironing it in place on the background block and hand appliqué it in place.*

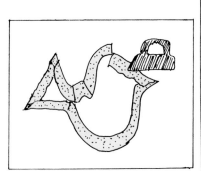

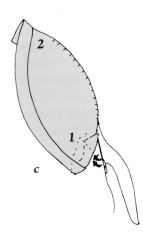

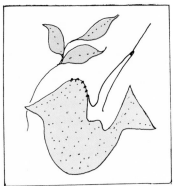

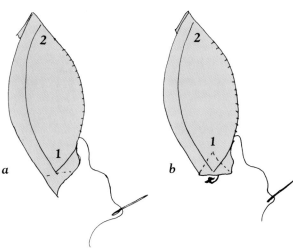

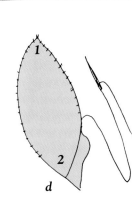

10. *Hand appliquéing a leaf.* **a:** *Beginning on a side, about ½" from a point, turn under the seam allowance and tack in place until you are about ½" from the next point.* **b:** *Fold under the seam allowance at the point so the point of the leaf lies on the base of a triangle that is turned under; finger press it in place.* **c:** *With the side of your needle, tuck under the remaining right seam allowance and tack it in place. Tuck under the left seam allowance at the first point (1) and tack it in place. Then rotate your work (**d**) so the unfinished seam allowance is at your right, and tack down the side seam until you are about ½ inch away from the second point of the leaf (2).* **e:** *fold up the second corner as you did for the first corner, and tuck the seam allowance to the right of the point in place. Then tack it. Tuck the seam allowance at the left of the point in place, and finish tacking around the point to complete the leaf (**f**).*

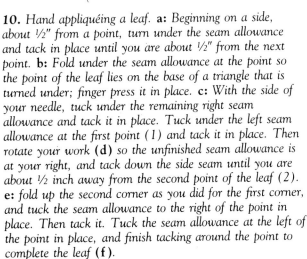

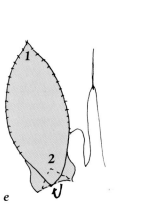

Turning Under Sharp Points

Leaves are frequently features of appliqué designs, and the sharp points they have need special attention for turning seam allowances. For hand appliqué, beginning on a side, about ½″ from a point, turn under the seam allowance and tack in place until you are about ½″ from the next point (Figure 10a). (If your leaf tips are very narrow, you may need to trim your seam allowances narrower before you tuck them in, to about ⅛″.) Fold under the seam allowance at the point so the point of the leaf lies on the base of a triangle that is turned under (Figure 10b); finger press it in place. With the side of your needle, tuck under the remaining right seam allowance and tack it in place (Figure 10c). Tuck under the left seam allowance at the first point (1) and tack it in place. Then rotate your work so the unfinished seam allowance is at your right, and tack down the side seam until you are about ½″ away from the second point of the leaf (2) (Figure 10d). Fold up the second corner as you did for the first corner (Figure 10e), and tuck the seam allowance to the right of the point in place. Then tack it. Tuck the seam allowance at the left of the point in place, and finish tacking around the point to complete the leaf (Figure 10f).

HAND APPLIQUÉ STITCHES

Basic Tacking Stitch

Select hand sewing thread, preferably 100% cotton, to match the appliqué piece. This is thinner than regular sewing thread and so is more easily hidden. If you can't find the exact color, a grayed or slightly darker version of the appliqué color is usually good. Cut an 18″ piece of thread. Run the thread through your beeswax to keep it from tangling. Knot the thread and sew through the back of the block; bring the needle up just under the folded edge of the seam allowance. Taking the smallest stitch possible, take the thread down immediately in front of the place you came up, over and perpendicular to the edge of the appliqué, going into the block. The needle next comes up through the appliqué, just under the fold of the seam allowance as before, ⅛ inch or less from the previous stitch (see diagram). Thus the distance traveled on the back of the block, and the tacking stitch that holds the appliqué is very tiny (see Figure 11). Many hand sewers like to appliqué towards themselves, with the thumb of the nonsewing hand pressing down and holding the seam allowance as the sewing hand works; it can pull your appliqué back a bit so you can stitch into the underside of the seam allowance for totally hidden stitches. Experiment and see which way works best for you.

Decorative Hand Appliqué Stitches

Patterns such as Sunbonnet Babies were often sewn down using a decorative buttonhole or blanket stitch to outline the pieces. A thread heavier than hand-sewing thread, such as crochet cotton or three strands of embroidery floss, was used to execute the decorative stitch, so that it would stand out and frame the appliqué. Choose a color of thread that contrasts with the appliqué, and attach the appliqué with the buttonhole stitch or blanket stitch; the blanket stitch is simply the buttonhole stitch done with the stitches spaced further apart (see Figure 12).

MACHINE APPLIQUÉ STITCHES

The satin stitch is the stitch most commonly used for machine appliqué, and is described below. If you plan to use other stitches, it is best to add seam allowances on your appliqué pieces when you cut them, and turn

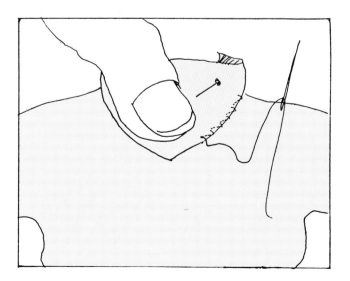

11. *The tacking stitch, hand appliqué. The needle comes up through the background fabric and through the seam allowance and top layer of the appliqué just under the seam allowance fold of the appliqué. The needle goes down into the background fabric right next to where it came up. The "traveling" (dashed line) is done underneath the two fabrics, and you emerge again in the appliqué seam allowance, just below the fold of the seam allowance. (You are sewing towards yourself; the thumb of the holding hand pushes the appliqué in so that a bit of the seam allowance underneath shows and you can stitch into it.) About 7 to 10 stitches to the inch is sufficient, or every ⅛″ (.3 cm).*

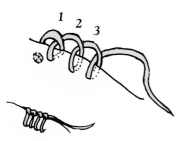

12. *Closeup of blanket stitches (widely spaced) and buttonhole stitches (close together).*

the seam allowances under, because other stitches won't protect the appliqué edge from fraying.

Position each appliqué piece in its proper place on the background block. If you are not using fusible webbing, baste, pin, or fabric glue each piece in position onto the background block. If you are using fusible webbing, fuse the pieces in place, starting with the layer that is directly touching the background block and working up.

Straight Stitching

For this method, you can use thread to match each appliqué color or you can use nylon thread, which will be almost invisible. If you use nylon thread, fill the bobbin with regular sewing thread. Set the stitch length for 8 to 10 stitches to the inch. Position the appliqué so that the needle just catches the edge of the fabric. Sew it in place. If your sewing machine has the capability, you could also use a hemstitch or blindstitch to sew down the appliqué.

Satin Stitch

With the satin stitch, you may be able to cut the appliqué without seam allowances, as the closely spaced stitches cover the raw edge. This depends on your sewing machine; the newer models can do much finer satin stitch than the older ones. Set the machine for satin stitch; do a test stitch on some scrap fabric to get the correct width and length of stitch for the effect you want. The wider stitch, the more prominent the stitching will be. The idea is to hide the raw edge of the appliqué, so it will look pretty and to prevent fraying of the fabric. If you want a really thin line of stitching, I would recommend that you cut your appliqués with a seam allowance.

To prevent puckering of the background fabric when satin stitching, place a sheet of tear-away stabilizer or tracing paper under the block. Sew through the stabilizer and when the sewing is complete, tear it away.

To execute a smooth inward curve, stop the machine frequently with the needle in the appliqué fabric

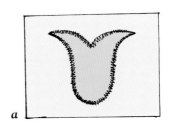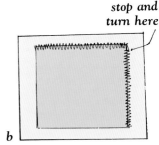

13. *Machine appliqué, using satin stitch.* **a:** *Taper the width of the stitch before a point and gradually increase it again after the point.* **b:** *To stitch a corner, stop stitching a bit before the corner with the needle in the background fabric, and turn the fabric. Then resume stitching.*

and turn the block slightly. For an outward curve, stop the machine with the needle in the background fabric and turn the block.

When sewing leaves or other tapering shapes, as you come to the point, gradually decrease the width of the satin stitch until you reach the point. With the needle down in the background block, rotate the fabric to its new position; gradually increase the stitch width as you sew away from the point on the other side (Figure 13a).

To turn a right-angle corner, stitch up to a short distance before the corner and stop, with the needle down in the background fabric; then rotate the block until you are lined up to sew the second side of the angle (Figure 13b).

STEMS AND VINES

Stems and vines are used frequently in appliqué designs. If the pattern has straight stems, the fabric can be cut on the straight grain of the fabric. For curved stems, you will need bias strips. When cloth is cut on the bias, it is more easily stretched, making it easier to form into smooth, flat curves. Purchased bias tape can be used, but it is more economical—and easier to get the exact color you want—if you make your own bias strips, as described below. These may be used for either hand or machine appliqué.

Cutting Bias Strips

To cut bias strips, take an on-grain square of fabric and spread it out on a flat surface. Fold the upper left corner down on the diagonal until the left edge of the fabric lines up with the lower edge of the fabric (Figure 14a). The diagonal fold is the bias of the fabric, 45° from the straight grain. Press the fold and cut along the fold. Measure out the needed width of your bias strip per-

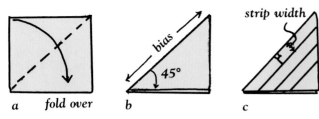

14. *Cutting bias strips.* **a:** *Fold the square in half on the diagonal so its long side is the bias of the fabric* **(b).** **c:** *Cut strips whose sides are parallel to the bias fold, of whatever strip width you need.*

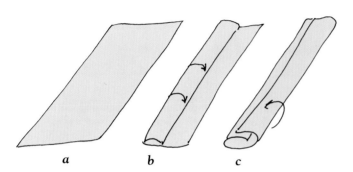

15. *Making bias strips, Method 1.* **a:** *The strip is right-side up.* **b:** *Fold one raw edge in.* **c:** *Fold the second raw edge in so its raw edge is short of the outside fold.*

pendicular to the cut edge and mark the other long side of your bias strip (Figure 14c). Cut the strip. Continue cutting as many strips as you need. I usually cut a long strip and trim it to the necessary length just before I apply it to the block.

Preparing and Applying Bias Strips

Preparing and Applying the Bias Strips: Method 1.
Cut a bias strip three times wider than the finished width of the stem (Figure 15a). With the right side of fabric facing out, fold one long raw edge in to the center of the strip (Figure 15b). Press. Fold the second long raw edge over so its raw edge is just short of the first fold (Figure 15c). Press. Turn the strip over and press it again on the top, but do not push the iron along the strip; just set it down, then pick up the iron and move it to the next section. Pushing the iron will stretch the strip. Baste the strip in place with its raw edges face-down on the block.

Preparing and Applying the Bias Strips: Method 2.
This method is suitable for very thin stems. Mark the stem position on the background fabric. Cut a bias strip four times as wide as the width of the finished stem. Fold the strip in half on its length, with the right side

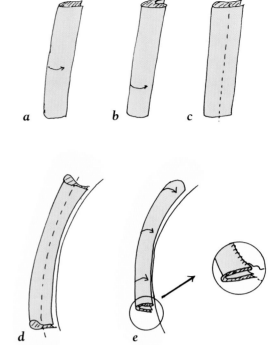

16. *Making bias strips, Method 2.* **a:** *Fold the strip in half on its length and press.* **b:** *Fold on its length again, press, and open the second fold out again.* **c:** *Stitch together the edges of the bias strip on the most recently made fold line.* **d:** *Stitch the bias strip in place with the raw edges on the guideline.* **e:** *Fold over the unattached (folded) long edge, and tack or machine stitch it in place.*

of the fabric facing outwards (Figure 16a). Press the fold to make a crease. Fold the strip in half on its length again, and press the fold (Figure 16b). Open out the second fold. The crease you made when you pressed the strip the second time is your sewing line (Figure 16c). To apply the bias strip, lay the raw edges of the folded strip along the guideline for the stem. Keep the raw edges of the strip even with the guideline, and sew along the crease by machine or by hand, using a small running stitch (Figure 16d). Then fold the loose long edge of the strip over again along the sewing line and bring the fold over the raw edge along the guideline (Figure 16e). Be sure the raw edges of the strip are covered. Appliqué stitch the fold in place along the guideline.

Preparing and Applying Bias Strips: Method 3. Cut a bias strip to a width two times plus ½″ wider than the finished appliqué. (For example, if you need a finished appliqué of ½″ width, cut a bias strip that is 1½″ wide.) Fold it in half on its length, with the right side of the fabric facing out (Figure 17a), pin the long edges together, and stitch the raw edges together ¼″ in from

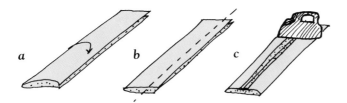

17. *Making bias strips, Method 3.* **a:** *Fold the cut strip in half, right-side out.* **b:** *Stitch ⅛ inch (.3 cm) in from the raw edge.* **c:** *Bring the seam allowances to the center of the strip and press.*

the edge (Figure 17b). (This may be done by machine, regardless of whether you will do machine or hand appliqué.) Center the seam allowances on the width of the strip and press them (Figure 17c). Trim the seam allowance back to ⅛″ if they extend beyond the edges of the strip. The strip is now ready to apply to your design, with the seam allowance facing the block fabric. The pressing task may be made easier by inserting a bias press strip or bias bar (a long strip of heat-resistant plastic) into the strip after you sew the long edge. Fold the seam allowance under the strip and press the whole unit. Press strips are sold at quilting stores and are available in varying widths. Choose a strip that is just a bit narrower than the width of your finished stem, so it will fit in easily.

CIRCLES

It is often difficult to turn under and sew the seam allowances of circles evenly and smoothly. The following method will give you perfectly round circles every time. Trace a circle of the correct size onto template cardboard, and cut it out. Using the template, trace and cut out your fabric appliqué circle, adding a ¼″ (.6 cm) seam allowance around the template circle as you go (Figure 18a). Run a line of basting stitches around the edge of the fabric circle, about ⅛ inch (.3 cm) in from the edge (Figure 18b), leaving a 2″ tail of thread at the start. Next, center the cardboard template in the middle of the fabric circle, on the wrong side of the fabric. Pull the basting thread up tightly around the template (Figure 18c). Press. Remove the template and tie the basting thread to hold the seam allowances in place. Sew the circle in place on the block.

REDUCING APPLIQUÉ THICKNESS

If the finished appliqués are several layers thick, you may find that it is very difficult to quilt through them.

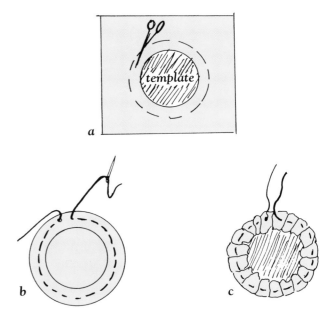

18. *Preparing circles for appliqué.* **a:** *Mark and cut out the fabric circle, adding a seam allowance.* **b:** *Run a line of basting ⅛ inch in from the raw edge.* **c:** *Reposition the template on the wrong side of the fabric and pull the basting stitches to fit the fabric around the template; then press.*

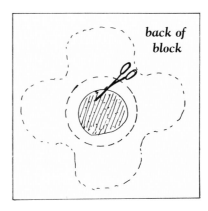

19. *Reducing the thickness of an appliqué. The shaded area is cut out of the background fabric and removed.*

To solve this problem, turn the quilt block over to its back and, using a pair of embroidery scissors or special appliqué scissors, trim away the center of the background fabric that lies immediately underneath the appliquéd area (Figure 19). Be sure to leave at least ¼″ (.6 cm) uncut between the stitching of the appliqué to the background and the cut edge, to be sure that the background fabric doesn't unravel. Where there are several layers of appliqué, some of the bulk of the bottom layer of appliqué (where it is covered by another layer) may be reduced in the same way.

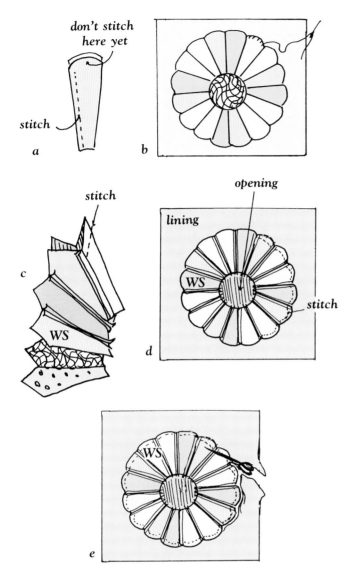

20. *Dresden Plate.* **a:** *Stitching together the round-ended segments.* **b:** *Appliquéing the round-ended plate to the background block.* **c:** *Hemming the edges of the angular segments.* **d:** *Stitching a round-ended "plate" to a square of lining fabric.* **e:** *Trimming off the excess lining fabric.*

DRESDEN PLATE

The Dresden Plate pattern is given in three versions in the pattern section of the book: with rounded segments, with angular segments, and in a version that uses both types of segments; the latter is generally known as Fancy Dresden Plate. The pattern is given without seam allowances; add ¼″ seam allowances around all pieces before cutting. The number of seg-

ments can vary from 12 to 16. The pattern is usually made up as a scrap design, but you can use a planned color scheme if you desire. Stitch the individual sections to each other with right sides of fabric facing (Figure 20a) and ¼″ seam allowances, but do not stitch into the curved (or pointed) top seam allowance. Press the joined seam allowances of the segments open to reduce bulk.

The plate is then appliquéd to a background block (Figure 20b). For the angular version of Dresden Plate, you can turn under the seam allowances of the points after you have stitched the segments together and before appliquéing as follows: Select one of the angular segments and fold it in half down the middle, with right sides of fabric facing (Figure 20c). Sew along the top seamline from the side seam to the point with ¼″ seam allowances. Trim the seam allowances, turn the segment right-side out and press. Repeat this process for all angular segments of the angular version. Then appliqué the entire plate in place as a unit, appliquéing on the center circle last (see earlier instructions on preparing a circle appliqué).

The traditional way of attaching the Dresden Plate is to baste it to the background block and turn under each segment's outer edge as you come to it, stitching it in place with tacking stitches. Here's an alternative to the usual method of turning under seam allowances on the versions of Dresden Plate that have curves on the outer edge of the segments. The method that follows, although it does use more fabric than other methods, makes the job easier. It is done after the individual segments of the plate are assembled, but before the center circle is added. Cut a square of lining fabric bigger than the circle formed by the assembled plate. Since this fabric square will not show, it is a good place to use up some of those ugly pieces of fabric you know you will never use in any of your quilts.

Lay the assembled plate right-side down on top of the lining fabric square. Following the seam lines, stitch all around the outside edge of the plate (Figure 20d). Trim off the excess lining fabric, even with the plate's edges. Clip the seam allowances at the curves and trim the seam allowances to reduce bulk. Turn the entire plate right-side out by pulling the lining fabric through the hole in the center of the plate. Smooth out the seams and press. Trim away excess lining fabric in the center circle and appliqué the plate to the background block. Appliqué the center circle over the plate after turning under the circle's seam allowance.

ADVANCED APPLIQUÉ TECHNIQUES

STUFFED APPLIQUÉ

Padding or stuffing areas of the design with loose batting is the most common way of adding depth to your block. There are several methods that can be used to accomplish this.

Method 1

Sew the appliqué in place as usual. Turn the block over to the back and carefully cut a small slit in the background block fabric only, in the center of the appliqué you want to stuff. (You will have your appliqué stitches to guide you.) Insert loose batting through the slit, pushing it into the space between the background and appliqué fabrics until you achieve the effect you want. Do not overstuff the appliqué or you will distort the background block. A blunt needle, a knitting needle, or a pencil back is helpful in pushing the stuffing exactly where you want it to be (Figure 21). Sew up the slash in the back with a whipstitch when you are done stuffing.

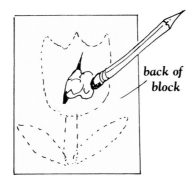

21. *Stuffing an appliqué from the back through a slit in the background fabric, which is later stitched closed.*

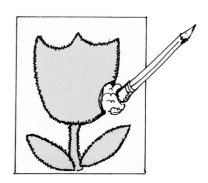

22. *Stuffing an appliqué from the front through an open appliqué seam.*

Method 2

Sew the appliqué in place, leaving an opening of ½″ to 1″ (1.3 to 2.5 cm) as you come to the end of the stitching. Insert batting through the opening, tamping it into any corners and distributing it evenly, until you have reached the thickness you want (Figure 22). Sew the opening closed.

Method 3

This method is especially useful when stuffing a large appliqué piece. Cut a sheet of batting in the shape of the appliqué, but slightly smaller all around. You can cut one or two layers of batting, depending on the depth you want to create. Position the batting on the block front, lay the appliqué over the batting, face up, and baste everything in place. Sew the appliqué down.

SHADOW APPLIQUÉ

This appliqué technique imparts a soft, shimmery, muted finish to the appliqué. It is achieved by placing

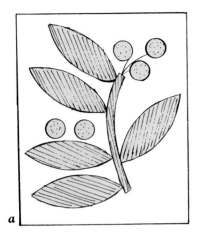 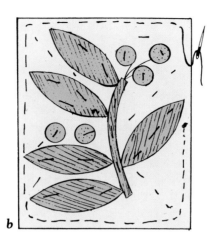 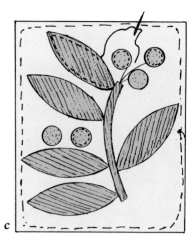

*23. Shadow appliqué. **a:** The appliqué pieces glued in place on their block. **b:** Translucent layer of fabric basted over the block. **c:** Individual appliqué pieces are sewn through all three layers in the running stitch.*

a square of translucent fabric such as organza or voile over the appliqué block. The fabrics chosen for the appliqué shapes should be fairly bright, because the overlay will mute the colors. The appliquéing and quilting are best done by hand. Proceed as follows:

1. Cut out the background block of fabric, with seam allowances added. Press the block in quarters or eighths to make fold lines to aid appliqué positioning. If necessary, trace the outline of the pattern lightly onto the background block to aid you in placing the appliqués.

2. Then cut the appliqué shapes out of their respective fabrics, without seam allowances, and glue them in place on the background block with fabric glue (Figure 23a) Extend any edges of shapes that will be overlapped by about ⅛″ before cutting. (You may cut the reversed appliqué shapes out of fusible webbing, fuse the webbing shapes to the wrong side of the appliqué fabric that is needed for each appliqué shape, cut them out of the appliqué fabrics, and fuse them in place with an iron on the front of the block instead of using glue.)

3. Cut a block of translucent fabric such as voile or organza the size of the background block plus seam allowance. Position the translucent block over the appliqué block and baste overall and around the outer edges of the block to hold it in place (Figure 23b). Cut and baste one translucent square for each shadow appliqué block.

4. Sew the appliqués on with hand running stitches all around their shapes through all three layers of

fabric (translucent fabric, appliqué, and backing), just inside the cut edges of the appliqués (Figure 23c). With a washable pen or pencil, mark quilting lines around your appliqués, in whatever design you like.

5. Prepare all the shadow blocks in your project the same way as described in steps 1–4. Cut any plain setting blocks out of the backing fabric, if you are using setting blocks around the shadow blocks, and mark their quilting lines also. Baste and sew the quilt blocks together to form the quilt top, first in rows, then joining the rows together, in the usual way.

6. Lay out your quilt backing and batting, and put the quilt top face up over them, and baste the three layers together in the usual way.

7. To quilt, follow the lines you have drawn on your quilt blocks, and quilt through all the layers, one block at a time, starting in the center of the quilt.

CREATING NEW PATTERNS

Once you have completed several appliqué blocks, I'm sure you will be ready to try your hand at designing your own block. Don't be timid. Remember, the vast majority of the quiltmakers featured in the Quiltmakers' Gallery have no formal art training, and many of them deny any artistic talent. (Well, we know they have talent, although it may not be drawing talent.) The nice thing about appliqué is that anything and everything can be turned into a pattern. Here are some suggestions to get you started.

Rearrange the elements in some of the blocks in this

book. See how many different ways you can arrange the various appliqué pieces to come up with new designs. Combine elements from two or three blocks to create a new one.

Children's coloring books are ideal sources for patterns. The pictures are simple line drawings that can be used as is, or enlarged or reduced to fit your needs. Children's books are also useful sources of design ideas. Many of the pictures are simple line drawings with color added. Select a picture you like and enlarge it, using a photocopy machine or by the grid method (making a grid of small squares on the original picture, drawing a grid of enlarged squares on a separate paper, and copying the design onto the enlarged grid, square by square). If the pattern is too detailed, eliminate some of the detail on your enlargement. To do this, draw around the outline, then draw in lines to delineate the major sections of the picture.

Adapt patterns from other forms of needlework. Embroidery, needlepoint, and cross-stitch patterns are easy to convert to appliqué patterns. In many instances, embroidery patterns can be used as is. At other times, you may want to enlarge a pattern and eliminate some of the detail. To convert a cross-stitch or needlepoint design, trace around the outer edge of the pattern. Add a few detail lines to fill out the shape.

There are many, many books available with patterns for decorative painting. These make great appliqué patterns. In fact, check out the patterns provided for other crafts, also. Woodburning and stained glass come quickly to mind as sources that can be adapted to appliqué quilting.

Garden books and catalogs are picture sources for fruit, vegetables, and flowers. You don't need to make an exact botanical copy. All you need do is convey the impression of a particular flower or fruit, so eliminate any unnecessary detail.

Artwork of all kinds should be studied for design ideas. In fact, all printed material can provide fodder for your quiltmaking. After all, professional artists compose not only fine art paintings, they also design packages and advertisements; almost everything in print was designed by an artist.

Explore your surroundings. Wallpaper may inspire a new design. Fran Soika, one of the quilters in the Quiltmakers' Gallery, translated the carpet pattern in her bedroom into a matching quilt. I once used cookie cutters to create a winter scene for a set of placemats.

Nola Eschedor, creator of the beautiful *Creatures of the Night* quilt in the Quiltmakers' Gallery, describes her creative process:

> I started out as a traditional quilter, using familiar patterns from books on quilting. I then decided to try an appliquéd pattern and realized the versatility and potential of this technique.
>
> Animals and children are my favorite subjects. I was born and raised in rural Wisconsin and nostalgic memories have inspired some of my designs. Greeting cards, children's books, quilting magazines and suggestions from family and friends also present interesting themes for a quilt design. Fabrics have always drawn my attention. The black fabric with the gold stars [used in *Creatures of the Night*] speaks of a night scene and a perfect background for nocturnal creatures.
>
> I draw out my full-sized patterns on graph paper. Children's coloring books are a great source of designs. Then I go through my stash of fabrics and pull out those which seem appropriate for the effect I have in mind. My fabric collection includes many patterns of texture and color variations. I select the fabrics as I go. The process is similar to painting a picture. When the appliquéd designs are complete, I work out sashings and borders to complete the quilt top. I achieve a great deal of satisfaction from knowing my quilts are original and unique and entirely my own creation.

Closeup of block from Nola Eschedor's Creatures of the Night.

Open your eyes and heart to the world around you and attune yourself to the creative forces within you. Once you embark on this grand adventure, you will never run out of ideas for quilts that are uniquely your own.

HELPFUL INFORMATION

CALCULATING QUILT SIZE AND BLOCKS NEEDED

The patterns provided do not give a suggested quilt size, just the final block size. The following section shows the process by which you can plan your quilt and arrive at the final quilt size.

To determine quilt size, several factors must be taken into account. Mattress size is your first consideration. Then, do you want the quilt to fall to the floor as a bedspread, with tuck-in for the pillows (which would add 18″ to 20″ to the length), or just as a cover for the mattress? Does the style of the bed present limitations? I have an antique bed with sideboards measuring 14″ deep. I don't want the quilt to fall below the sideboards, so I am limited in the amount of overhang. A throw for the couch would be smaller, as would a baby quilt.

As a general guideline, mattress sizes* are as follows:

California King	72″ × 84″
King	76″ × 80″
Queen	60″ × 80″
Double	53″ × 74.5″ (appx. 75″)
Twin	38″ × 75″
Cot	30″ × 75″
Crib	27″ × 52″

It's a good idea to go ahead and measure your mattress, especially if it suffers from middle-age spread. Measure from side-to-side to obtain width, and from top-to-bottom for length.

For a double-size bed, my calculations would be as follows:

Mattress size:	53″ wide × 75″ long
Allowance for pillows:	18″
Overhang at foot:	12″
Overhang on each side:	
12″ × 2 sides =	24″
Totals	77″ wide × 105″ long

The next example is for a modern bed, with a double-size mattress. Mattress and box springs have a depth of 14″ and the quilt will not cover the pillows:

Mattress size:	53″ wide × 75″ long
Overhang at foot:	14″
Overhang on each side:	
14″ × 2 =	28″
Totals	81″ wide × 89″ long

You may want your quilt to extend further, of course.

Once you've decided how large you want the quilt, it's time to determine what size block you will use. You should be flexible in this area, because the finished quilt size usually will not come out evenly divisible by the block size. The following tables illustrate the problems that arise in arriving at an approximate quilt size of 77″ × 106″.

---

* U.S. mattress sizes are given here.

Various Block and Border* Combinations for a Quilt
Approximately 77″ × 106″

Block Size	Blocks Across	Blocks Down	Total Blocks Needed
8″	9 blocks = 72″ + 5″ border	12 blocks = 96″ + 10″ border	108
9″	8 blocks = 72″ + 5″ border	11 blocks = 99″ + 7″ border	88
10″	7 blocks = 70″ + 7″ border	10 blocks = 100″ + 6″ border	70
12″	6 blocks = 72″ + 5″ border	8 blocks = 96″ + 10″ border	48
14″	5 blocks = 70″ + 7″ border	7 blocks = 98″ + 8″ border	35
15″	5 blocks = 75″ + 2″ border	7 blocks = 105″ + 1″ border	35
15″	4 blocks = 60″ + 17″ border	6 blocks = 90″ + 16″ border	24
16″	4 blocks = 64″ + 13″ border	6 blocks = 96″ + 10″ border	24
18″	4 blocks = 72″ + 5″ border	5 blocks = 90″ + 16″ border	20

*The border allowance includes the width of both borders (two side borders or a top and a bottom border) to total 77″ × 106″.

As you can see, none of the block sizes will come out with the side borders of equal width to the top and bottom borders, although the 14″ block is close.

If you decide to use a 12″ block, you can either increase the side borders to equal 10″ or decrease the top and bottom border to total 5″, or choose some middle width for both, like 7″.

Setting the quilt with sashing strips is another very popular method of getting the quilt size you want. In fact, in the above examples, it would be easier to set the 18″ block this way, rather than try to adjust the borders to allow for an 11″ difference in the combined border widths of the two side borders vs. the combined width of the top and bottom borders. The following chart shows an example of the calculations and adjustments needed when using sashing. In the example, the quilt size is 77 × 106″, and border and sashing strips are of equal width to each other.

You could also use an intermediate block size (e.g. 12½″) by enlarging or reducing your patterns a bit, or adding more space around the block pattern.

The sashing strips in the second table could be increased to 5″ or 6″ in width, depending on the block size, or you could add an outer border if the quilt is still too small after these adjustments.

Blocks set on the diagonal must be multiplied by 1.42 to determine the finished width of each block. The following shows the width of the blocks and rounds it off to the nearest quarter inch.

8″ block = 11.36 or 11.5″
9″ block = 12.78 or 12.75″
10″ block = 14.2 or 14″
11″ block = 15.62 or 15.5″
12″ block = 17.04 or 17″
13″ block = 18.46 or 18.5″
14″ block = 19.88 or 20″
15″ block = 21.3 or 21.25″
16″ block = 22.72 or 22.75″
17″ block = 24.14 or 24″
18″ block = 25.56 or 25.5″

**Various Block and Sashing Strip Combinations for a Quilt
Approximately 77 × 106″***

Block Size	Blocks Across	Blocks Down	Total Blocks Needed

8″	8 blocks = 64″
	   nine 2″ strips = 18″
	Finished size: 82″ × 102″
		10 blocks = 80″
		   eleven 2″ strips = 22″
			80

9″	7 blocks = 63″
	   eight 2″ strips = 16″
	Finished size: 79″ × 110″
		10 blocks = 90″
		   ten 2″ strips = 20″
			70

10″	6 blocks = 60″
	   seven 3″ strips = 21″
	Finished size: 81″ × 107″
		8 blocks = 80″
		   nine 3″ strips = 27″
			48

12″	5 blocks = 60″
	   six 3″ strips = 18″
	Finished size: 78″ x 108″
		7 blocks = 84″
		   eight 3″ strips = 24″
			35

14″	4 blocks = 56″
	   five 3″ strips = 15″
	Finished size: 71″ × 105″
	(This size may be better if
	   set solid.)
		6 blocks = 84″
		   seven 3″ strips = 21″
			24

15″	4 blocks = 60″
	   five 3″ strips = 15″
	Finished size: 75″ × 93″
	*If the lattice strips are made 4″
	   wide:*five 4″ strips = 20″
	Finished size: 80″ × 99″
		5 blocks = 75″
		   six 3″ strips = 18″
		
		   six 4″ strips = 24″
			20

16″	4 blocks = 64″
	   five 4″ strips = 20″
	Finished size: 84″ × 104″
		5 blocks = 80″
		   six 4″ strips = 24″
			20

18″	3 blocks = 54″
	   four 4″ strips = 16″
	Finished size: 70″ × 114″
		5 blocks = 90″
		   six 4″ strips = 24″
			15

* Border is assumed to be same width as sashing here.

The foregoing may seem like a lot of unnecessary math, but some familiarity with it will be helpful to you. Before you can figure the amount of fabric to buy, you must know how many blocks you need to complete the quilt top. For a double bed, you can get some idea just by using the figures given here.

AMOUNT OF FABRIC NEEDED FOR APPLIQUÉS

Now that you know how many blocks you need, you can determine how much fabric will be required for the appliqués.

1. Count how many appliqué units of a particular fabric you need per block. For example, in block A there are 4 light pink tulip shapes that will be cut from the same fabric (Figure 24).

2. Multiply the number of units per block by the total number of blocks; for our purposes, let's assume the quilt has 35 blocks. That would mean we need 35 blocks × 4 tulips per block or 140 pink tulips for the quilt top.

3. Measure the tulip, add ¼″ seam allowances around it and determine from what size rectangle the tulip block could be cut. Let's say the tulip will fit on a 3″ × 5″ rectangle, including seam allowances.

4. Divide the *width* of the rectangle into the *width* of the fabric you have. In this case, let's say we have 45″-wide fabric. Then 45″ divided by 3″ = 15, so we know 15 tulips can be cut *across the width* of the fabric.

5. Divide the length of the appliqué's rectangle into one yard (36″) of fabric to calculate how many units will fit on one yard of fabric. In our example, that's 5″ divided into 36″ = 7; 7 tulip rectangles can be cut down the length of the fabric.

6. Multiply the number of units that can be cut across by the number of units that can be cut down the length of one yard (36″) to determine how many units can be cut from 1 yard of fabric (45″ × 36″). In our example, that's 15 units across × 7 down = 105 units per yard.

7. Divide the total number of units you need in the quilt top (calculated in step 2) by the number of units you get per yard to determine the total yardage required to make those units. In our case we need 140 of the tulips, but we get 105 per yard; 140 divided by 105 = about 1.3 yards; round up to about 1½ yards. We therefore need to get 1½ yards of fabric to make the tulip appliqués. Repeat this process to estimate the yardage for each appliqué fabric.

You also need background fabric of course, which can be calculated by multiplying the size of one block (adding in two inches on the sides for safety's sake) times the number of blocks in the quilt. Calculate how many blocks will fit across 45″. For example, if you need thirty-five 6″ × 8″ blocks, divide 45″ by 8 (6″ + 2″) to get 5; five blocks can be cut across the width of the fabric. To calculate what length of background fabric you need, take the length of the block, 8″, add some extra (2″) to get 10″ long. We will need 7 rows of blocks because we can only cut 5 across the fabric. Seven × 10″ per block length = 70″, or about 2 yards. We'll therefore need 2 yards of background fabric.

USING QUILTING PATTERNS

There are many stencils available for marking quilting designs onto your quilt top. Choose a design that won't overwhelm your appliqué patterns, but will harmonize with them. If you have solid blocks alternating with appliquéd blocks, you may want to pick up some of the appliqué designs to use as a quilting pattern in the solid blocks. Fabric marking pencils of a contrasting color to

24. *Block A, which has 4 tulip shapes (left). Right: the rectangle of appliqué fabric from which a tulip shape, inlcuding seam allowances, can be cut.*

your quilt block, tailor's chalk, or even soap slivers can be used to mark the quilt top. To trace a quilting pattern onto your quilt top, trace out the pattern onto paper in dark lines with an indelible pen. Place it under your fabric and trace the design onto your quilt top with a fabric marking pencil or other tool. If you have difficulty seeing the pattern, use a light box or tape the pattern and quilt top to a bright window pane and trace through.

The kind of batting you use in part determines how closely you need to space your quilting lines. Traditional cotton batting must be quilted with lines that are close together; polyester batting can be quilted with lines that are further apart. Choose a low-loft batting so that it is not difficult to quilt through.

The following section, Photographs of Appliqué Pattern Blocks, shows a full-color model for each appliqué pattern given in the book. See the pattern pages for patterns, block sizes, and other details.

Simple criss-cross quilting sets off this Rose Wreath from Cheryl Pedersen's Baltimore Sampler Quilt.

QUILTMAKERS' GALLERY

MEET THE QUILTMAKERS

Below are brief biographies of the women whose work is shown in the Quiltmakers' Gallery.

Leita Shahan: Leita has been quilting since 1975. In 1983, with the help of her parents, she opened a quilt shop. Her shop was very successful and Leita became an impassioned quilter. Her interest gradually zeroed in on miniature quilts. She lectures and teaches the making of miniatures and has entered and won several competitions. Leita's latest creation is a nine-block Sunbonnet Sue with blocks only 1″ high. She says the secret to success when working in a scale this small is *toothpicks*. It's the only way to turn under those minuscule seam allowances.

Fran Soika: Fran needs no introduction. Her quilts hang in galleries and private collections the world over. Fran's first quilt, in 1956, was for her daughter's room. She had no idea how to make a quilt. Only after completing her second appliqué quilt did she find any instructions on quiltmaking. She tried making a traditional quilt "by the book" and found it boring. She went back to using her own methods. Fran's work is constantly changing and evolving, reflecting whatever her current interests are. Her presidential quilts have attracted a great deal of interest. She recently completed the *Clinton Quilt*. Her love of the Southwest influenced her work for several years, but she has now turned her attention to interpreting Matisse in reverse appliqué. Fran is an outstanding lecturer and teacher, as well as a judge of quilting. If you ever have the chance to attend her class or lecture, don't miss it.

Ann Doherty: Ann is another avid quilter whose home is filled with quilts. Ann is an active member of the Cascade Quilt Guild, and when we visited her she had put aside her own quilting, and was working hard to finish a quilt for a fellow member who was quite ill.

Betty Nye: Betty's first quilt was *Victorian Ladies*, made in 1980, which has won several Viewer's Choice Awards. She is currently collecting fabric for a new version showing fashion through the ages. The *Heirloom Appliqué Quilt* was made in 1989 as an anniversary

Detail of Victorian Ladies, designed, appliquéd, and quilted by Betty Nye, 1980.

Above: Thunderbird, appliquéd and quilted by Anne Doherty, 1990. Design by Fran Soika, based on an old Pueblo Indian design.

present for her in-laws. In the planning stages is a very ambitious quilt depicting a Civil War battle. Her sister, who is an artist, drew up the battle scene and Betty is looking for the appropriate fabrics. She considers this a long-term project and when she finishes it, I'm sure it too will be a prize winner.

Cheryl Pedersen: Cheryl wears many hats in the quilt world, quiltmaker, shop owner, teacher, and judge. The quilt whose details are shown in the gallery section began as a Baltimore album quilt. When it was time to do the pictorial of a city landmark, Cheryl realized she knew absolutely nothing about Baltimore. Ever creative, she drafted a block depicting Cleveland's Terminal Tower. Now, she's not sure whether to call it a Baltimore Album Quilt or a Cleveland Album Quilt. By any name, it is a beautiful quilt.

Clare Murray: Clare's quilts are among those I selected that I would consider art quilts; that is, quilts made to be displayed as art rather than used in the traditional manner. I found the play of color and form so appealing I couldn't resist including them. Clare is a practicing artist and also teaches, both at the elementary school level and at the Canton Art Institute. Quilting is a medium through which she can express her artistic talents. First she designs and makes the background quilt. She embellishes the surface by lay-

Frog on a Lily Pad, designed, appliquéd, and quilted by Linda Smith Poole, 1991.

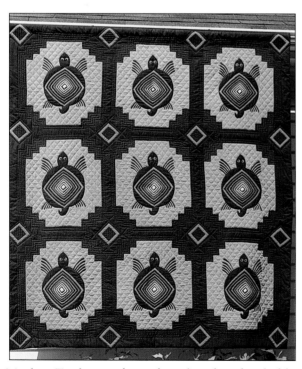

Mimbres Turtles was designed, appliquéd, and quilted by Fran Soika.

ering, painting, screen printing, and embroidery. Paint is applied with an atomizer. She quilts both by hand and machine. Obviously, a great deal of time and talent goes into the construction of her work.

Linda Poole: Linda has fun with quilts. When I received a letter from her mentioning her wall hanging *Frogmoor and the Blue Moose,* I had to find out the story behind the title. It turned out that Linda has an obsession with frogs. She's been collecting them for years in various art forms and her home is filled with frogs. Her passion is so complete that she has named her home Frogmoor. The Blue Moose is her blue Corvette.

Nola Eschedor: Nola began quilting when she retired four years ago. Even though she has no formal art training, most of her quilts are original designs. Nola loves both children and animals and they are frequently the theme of her quilts. *Creatures of the Night* is just one example of her outstanding design ability and the workmanship she puts into her quilts.

Edith Trocchio: Edith has been quilting for several years; her goal is to make a quilt for each of her grandchildren. She has already completed seven quilts and has three to go. Edith has made eleven of the *Santa Claus* wallhangings; even though they were made from a commercial pattern, she has made each one unique by her choice of color and fabric.

Irene Goodrich: Irene is an avid quilter who has been quilting for many years. The day we were in Columbus, plasterers had invaded her home so she brought her quilts over to The Quiltery for photographing. All of the designs are traditional patterns, and the workmanship is exquisite. Her quilts have won many ribbons in competitions.

Judy Smith: Judy is an art teacher as well as a quilting teacher. In fact, her life as a quilting teacher has been very exciting. Last year she travelled to Australia to teach a quilting seminar and is planning on returning again this year. Judy began with traditional patchwork, but felt there was something lacking in the finished quilt. She began adding surface appliqué to already completed patchwork pieces and felt them come alive. *Urban Garden* was her first design using this technique. Most of the design is regular appliqué, but the surprise touch is the use of purchased silk sunflowers. It's a perfect touch to add dimension to the surface.

Nancy Watts already had a BFA when she became interested in quilting. She was searching for an art form that used nontoxic materials so she could work while her small children were around, one that could be interrupted, if necessary. A friend taught her how to quilt, and she went on to join North Coast Needlers in Westlake, Ohio. Nancy sometimes hand paints and dyes fabrics to get the colors she needs. At times she starts with a color sketch and follows it closely; at other times the work grows and changes as she responds to the colors and textures before her.

Peggy Deierhoi: Peggy's passion is quilting. Her husband says she is obsessed with it; after touring her home, I can see what he means. Her home is a quilt lover's dream. Her quilts range from full-size to miniatures and she is constantly exploring and trying new techniques. I was especially taken with the design on the back of her Noah's Ark quilt: the ark resting on top of the mountain, which she designed herself. (The front design is a pattern from Red Wagon of Liberty, Missouri.)

Noah's Ark, appliquéd by Peggy Deierhoi, quilted by Nancy Watts, 1992–1993. Pattern by Red Wagon, Liberty, Missouri. At right: Detail of the quilt's back.

Homage to Georgia O'Keeffe III was designed, appliquéd, and quilted by Nancy L. Watts in 1993.

Detail of quilt.

Homage to Georgia O'Keeffe II was designed, appliquéd, and quilted by Nancy L. Watts in 1993.

Detail of quilt.

Exteriors #3, designed, appliquéd, and quilted by
Clare M. Murray, 1990.

Interior #3, designed, appliquéd, and quilted by
Clare M. Murray in 1980.

Birds of a Feather was designed, appliquéd, and quilted by Fran Soika.

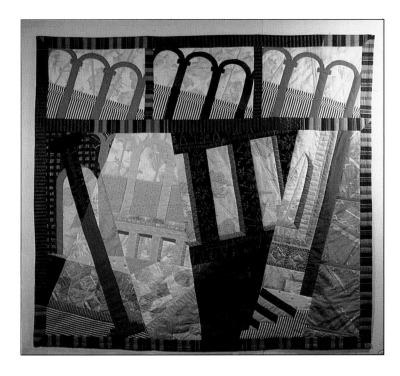

Exteriors #1, designed, appliquéd, and quilted by Clare M. Murray in 1990.

*Victorian Ladies, designed, appliquéd,
and quilted by Betty Nye, 1980.*

Detail of quilt.

Creatures of the Night, designed, appliquéd and quilted by Nola Eschedor, 1992. Below: details of quilt.

Miniature Hanover Tulip was appliquéd and quilted by Leita E. Shahan from a reduced version of Hanover Tulip, a pattern by Beverley Cosby.

Acoma was designed, appliquéd, and quilted by Fran Soika in 1988 from patterns based on traditional Acoma Indian pottery designs by Drew Lewis.

Urban Garden was designed, appliquéd, and quilted by Judith Kessler Smith in 1993.

Frogmoor and the Blue Moose was designed, quilted, and appliquéd by Linda Smith Poole in 1992.

Barnyard, designed, appliquéd and quilted by Nola
Eschedor, 1994.

Miniature Basket was appliquéd and quilted by Leita
E. Shahan in 1994 from a traditional design.

*Heirloom Appliqué, appliquéd and quilted by
Betty Nye in 1989; pattern by Pat Andreatta.*

*Images of Spain was designed, appliquéd, and
quilted by Fran Soika in 1993.*

Baltimore Sampler Quilt, appliquéd and quilted by Cheryl
Pedersen in 1991 from her original block designs and
others. See permissions for details.

Detail of Baltimore Sampler Quilt

Moss Rose, appliquéd and quilted by Irene Goodrich in
1988. Patterns by Nancy Cabot.

Detail (Chrysanthemum block).

Ruby S. McKim Flower Garden, appliquéd and quilted by Irene Goodrich in 1977, from patterns by Ruby Short McKim.

Detail (Nasturtium block).

I Remember Santa Skating on Mistletoe Pond was appliquéd and quilted by Edith Trocchio from a pattern by De Selby.

Peony, appliquéd and quilted by Linda Smith Poole in 1982 from a traditional design.

The following section, Photographs of Appliqué Pattern Blocks, shows a full-color model for each appliqué pattern given in the book. See the pattern pages for patterns, block sizes, and other details.

PHOTOGRAPHS OF APPLIQUÉ
PATTERN BLOCKS

Fleur de Lis #1
(pattern on page 65)

Fleur de Lis #2
(pattern on page 65)

Fleur de Lis #3
(pattern on page 66)

Fleur de Lis #4
(pattern on page 67)

Fleur de Lis #5
(pattern on page 67)

Fleur de Lis #6
(pattern on page 68)

Buckeye Blossom
(pattern on page 69)

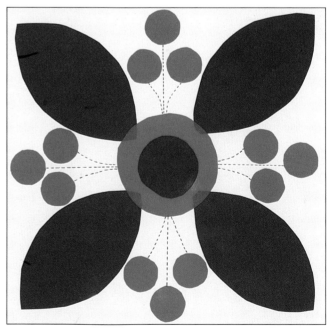

Hawthorne Berries
(pattern on page 70)

Tangerine
(pattern on page 71)

Marigold
(pattern on page 72)

Pumpkin Flower
(pattern on page 73)

Grape Wreath
(pattern on page 74)

Butterfly #1
(pattern on page 75)

Butterfly #2
(pattern on page 76)

Butterfly #3
(pattern on page 77)

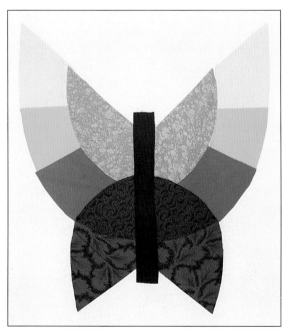

Butterfly #4
(pattern on page 78)

Butterfly #5
(pattern on page 79)

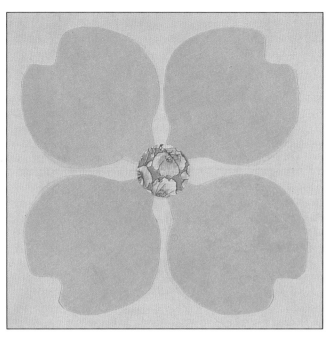

Dogwood
(pattern on page 80)

Buds and Blossoms
(pattern on page 81)

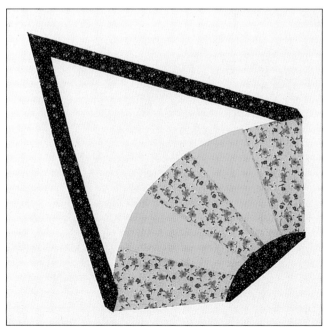

Colonial Basket
(pattern on page 82)

Basket #1
(pattern on page 83)

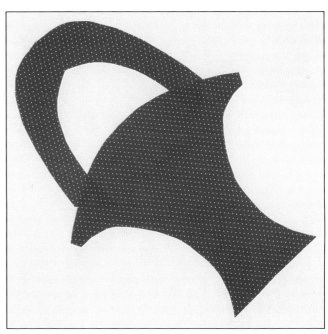

Basket #2
(pattern on page 84)

May Basket
(pattern on page 85)

Order #11
(pattern on page 87)

Reel
(pattern on page 88)

Grape Leaf and Reel
(pattern on page 87)

Oak Leaf and Reel
(pattern on page 88)

Calliope
(pattern on page 89)

Pinwheel and Oak Leaf
(pattern on page 90)

Sundew
(pattern on page 91)

Princess Feather
(patterns on pages 93–94)

Flowers in a Pot
(patterns on pages 95–96)

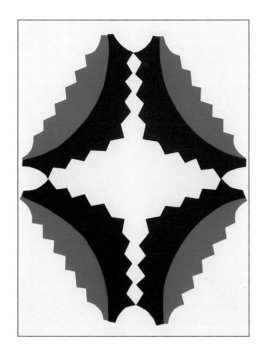

Stars in Red, White, and Blue Circles
(pattern on page 97)

Cherry Rose
(pattern on page 97)

Bow Knot
(pattern on page 98)

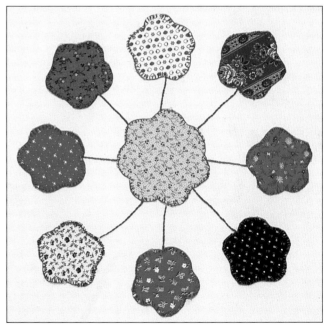

Ring Around the Posy
(pattern on page 99)

String of Beads
(pattern on page 100)

Zinnia
(pattern on page 100)

Prairie Flower
(pattern on page 101)

Angel's Trumpet
(pattern on page 102)

Christmas Cactus
(pattern on page 103)

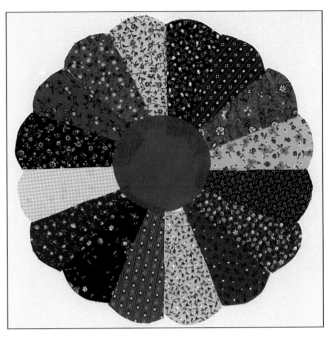

Dresden Plate I
(pattern on page 104)

Dresden Plate II
(pattern on page 104)

Fancy Dresden Plate
(pattern on page 104)

Friendship Dahlia
(pattern on page 105)

Pineapple #1
(pattern on page 106)

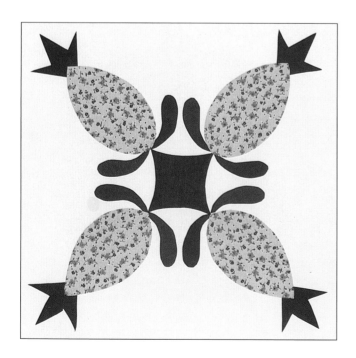

Pineapple #2
(pattern on page 107)

Indiana Rose
(pattern on page 108)

Lancaster Rose
(pattern on page 109)

Ohio Rose
(pattern on page 110)

Rose Cross
(pattern on page 111)

Ohio Rose Bush
(patterns on pages 112–113)

Lotus
(pattern on page 114)

Thistle
(pattern on page 115)

Cherry Tree
(patterns on pages 118–119)

Laurel Leaves
(pattern on page 116)

Clover
(pattern on page 116)

Oak Leaf and Acorns
(pattern on page 117)

Whirling Tulips
(pattern on page 120)

Tulips #1
(pattern on page 121)

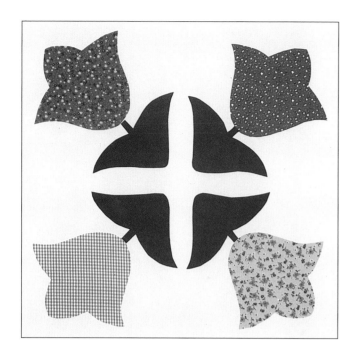

Tulips #2
(pattern on page 122)

Tulips #3
(pattern on page 123)

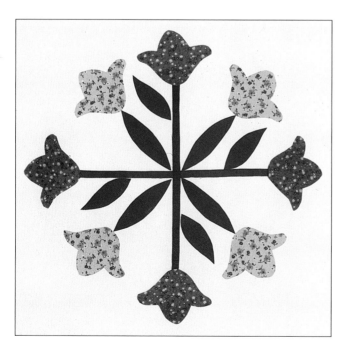

Crossed Tulips #1
(pattern on page 124)

Crossed Tulips #2
(pattern on page 125)

Rose and Tulip
(pattern on page 126)

Harrison Rose
(pattern on page 127)

Sunbonnet Sue #1
(pattern on page 128)

Sunbonnet Sue #2
(pattern on page 129)

Sunbonnet Sue #3
(pattern on page 130)

Overall Bill #1
(pattern on page 131)

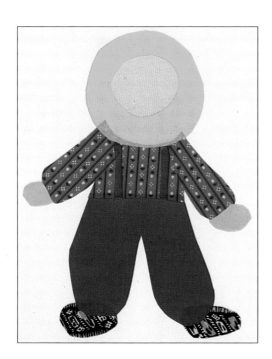

Overall Bill #2
(pattern on page 132)

Overall Bill #3
(pattern on page 133)

Wreath and Terminal Tower Building: designed, appliquéd, and quilted by Cheryl Pedersen of Novelty, Ohio, in her Baltimore Sampler Quilt, 1991 (pattern on pages 136, 137).

Princess Feather: from Baltimore Sampler Quilt by Cheryl Pedersen 1991, from a pattern published by the Kentucky Heritage Quilt Society of Lexington, Kentucky 1984 (pattern on page 135).

Pomegranate Block: from Baltimore Sampler Quilt, by Cheryl Pedersen from a pattern adapted by Irene S. Cook of Russell, Ohio from an antique quilt design (pattern on page 134).

Nasturtium: appliquéd and quilted by Irene Goodrich of Columbus, Ohio, in her Ruby Short McKim Flower Garden Quilt in 1977; pattern by Ruby Short McKim (pattern on page 140).

Tiger Lily: appliquéd and quilted by Irene
Goodrich of Columbus, Ohio, in her Ruby
Short McKim Flower Garden Quilt in
1977; pattern by Ruby Short McKim
(pattern on page 139).

Bleeding Heart: appliquéd and quilted by
Irene Goodrich of Columbus, Ohio, in her
Ruby Short McKim Flower Garden Quilt
in 1977; pattern by Ruby Short McKim
(pattern on page 141).

Chrysanthemum: appliquéd and quilted by
Irene Goodrich of Columbus, Ohio, in her
Ruby Short McKim Flower Garden Quilt
in 1977; pattern by Ruby Short McKim
(pattern on page 138).

APPLIQUÉ PATTERNS

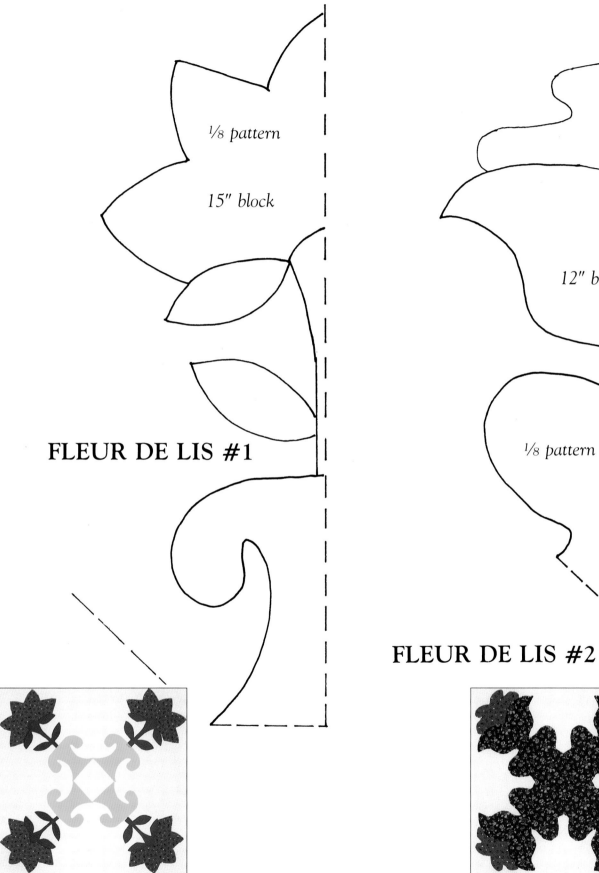

⅛ pattern

15" block

FLEUR DE LIS #1

12" block

⅛ pattern

FLEUR DE LIS #2

¼ pattern

FLEUR DE LIS #3

15″ block

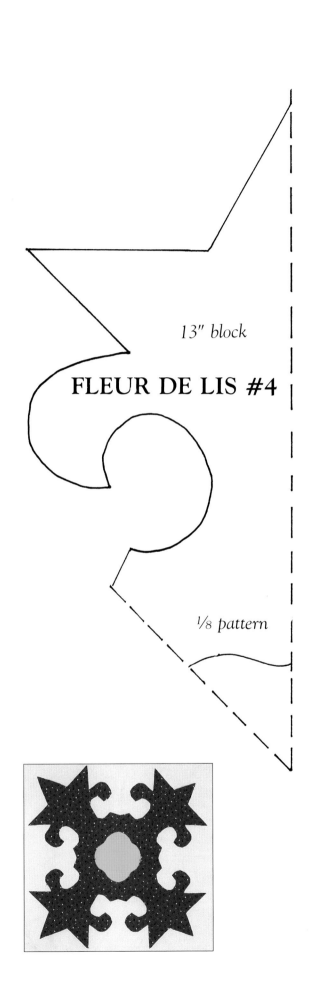

13″ block

FLEUR DE LIS #4

⅛ pattern

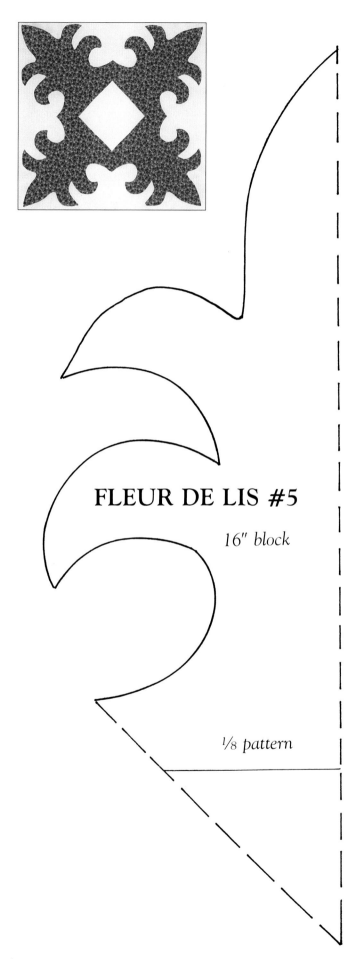

FLEUR DE LIS #5

16″ block

⅛ pattern

67

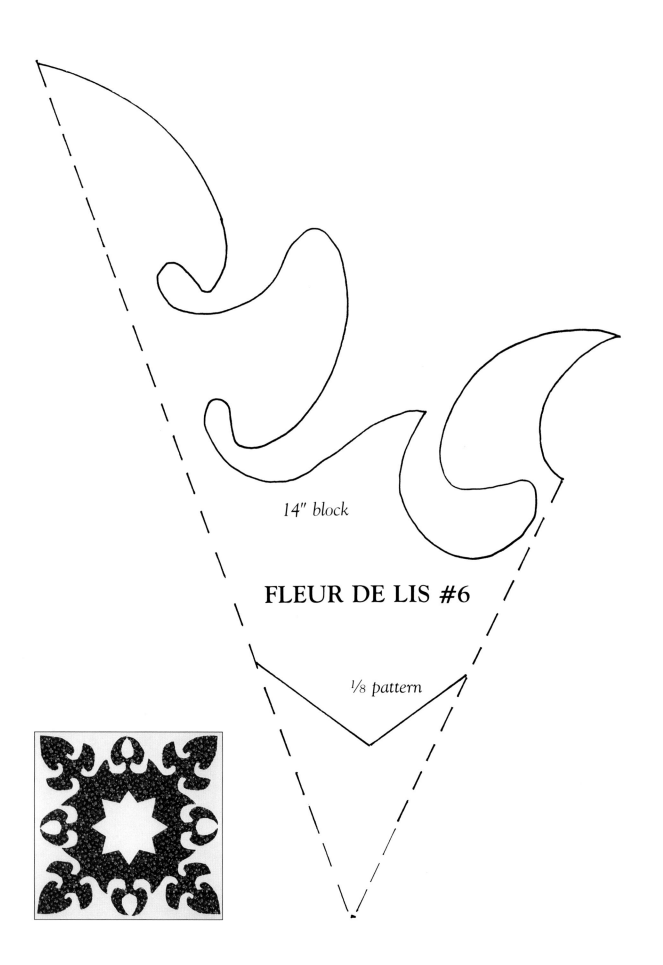

14" block

FLEUR DE LIS #6

¹/₈ pattern

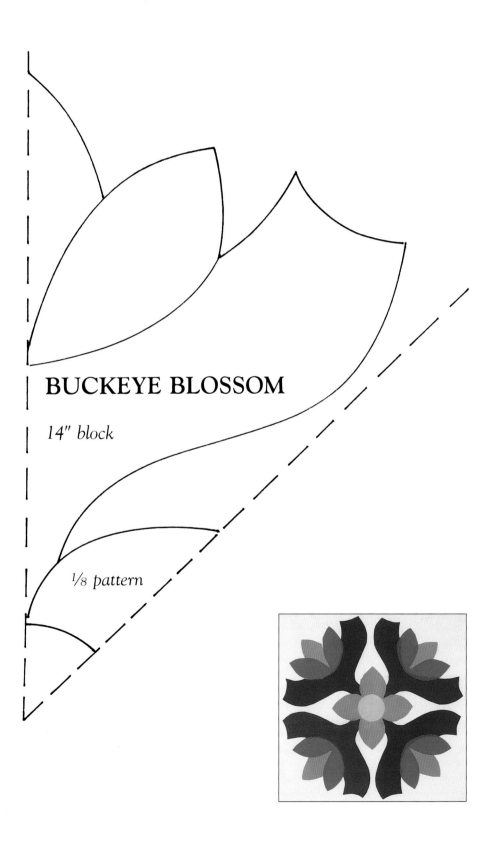

BUCKEYE BLOSSOM

14" block

⅛ pattern

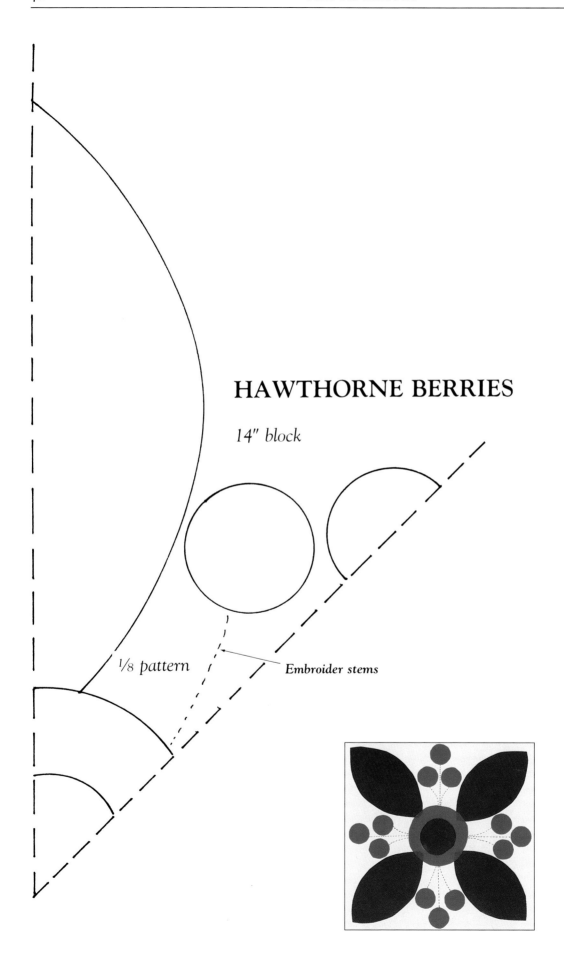

HAWTHORNE BERRIES

14" block

⅛ pattern

Embroider stems

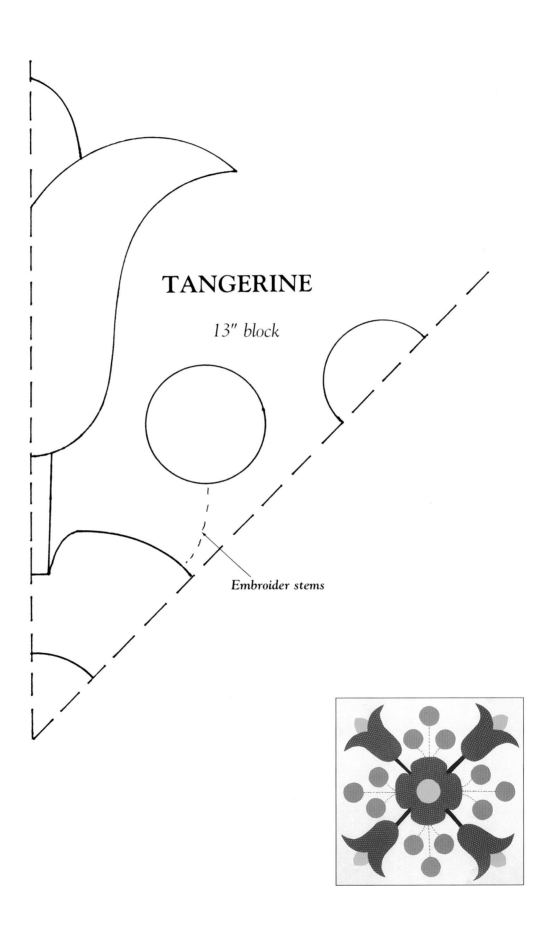

TANGERINE

13" block

Embroider stems

MARIGOLD

14" block

⅛ pattern

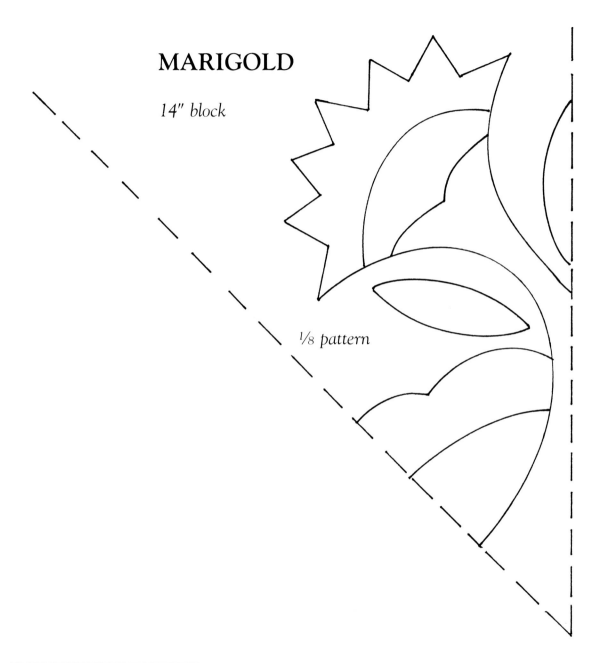

PUMPKIN FLOWER

14" block

⅛ pattern

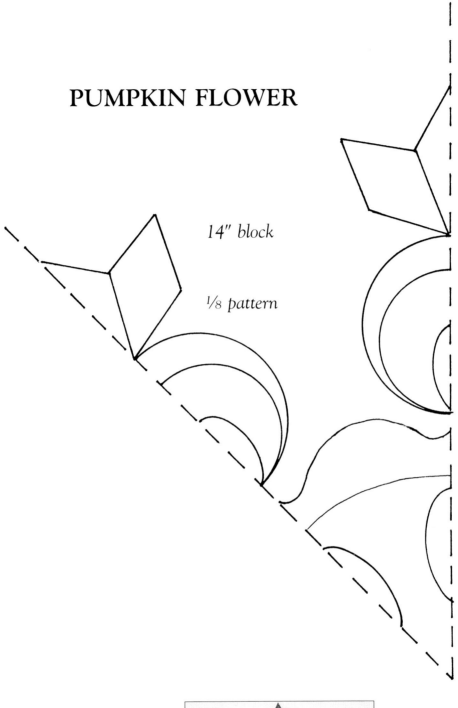

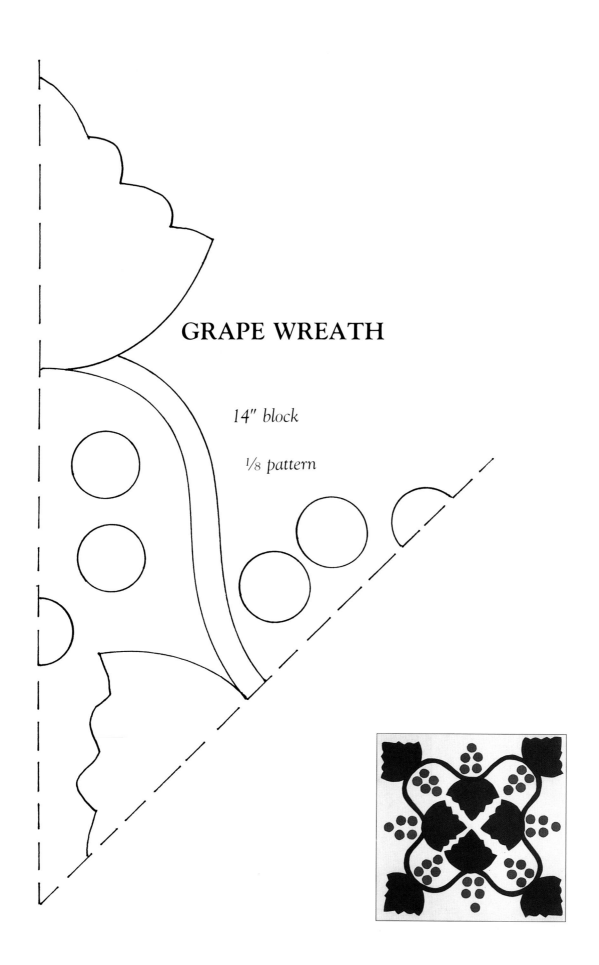

GRAPE WREATH

14" block

⅛ pattern

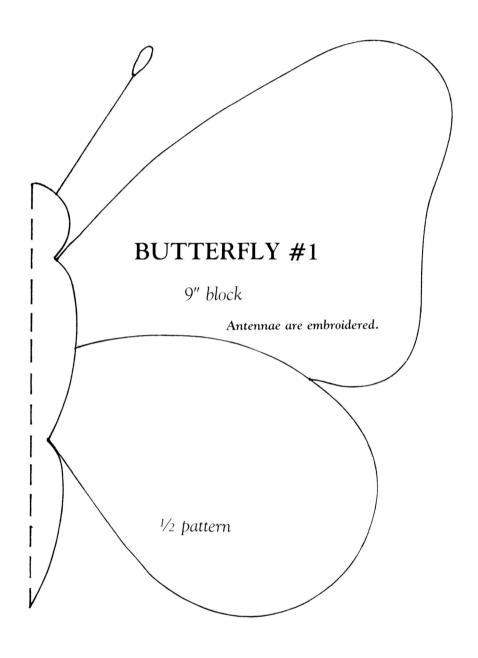

BUTTERFLY #1

9″ block

Antennae are embroidered.

½ pattern

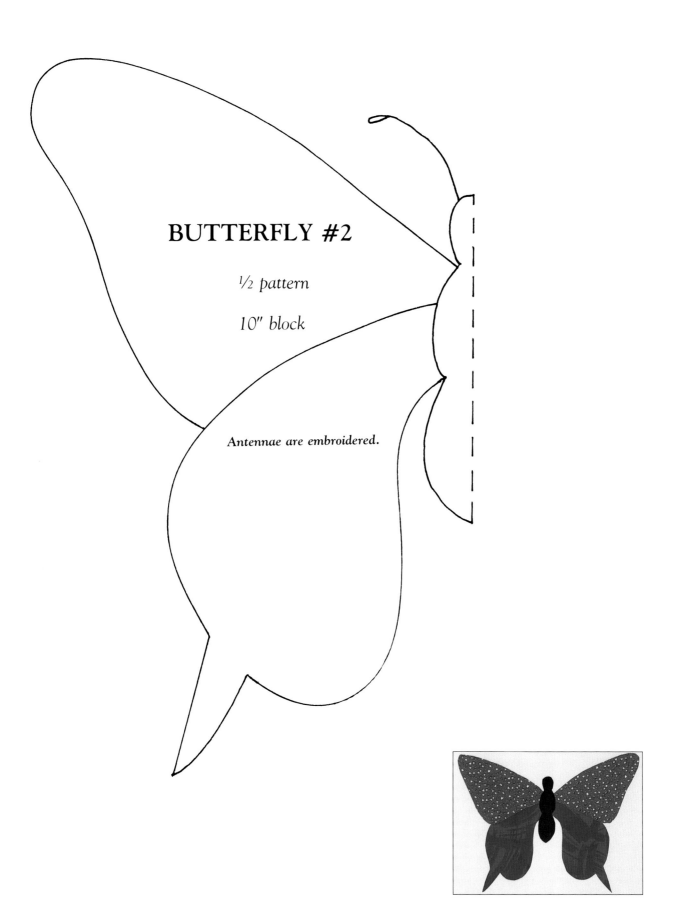

BUTTERFLY #2

¹/₂ pattern

10″ block

Antennae are embroidered.

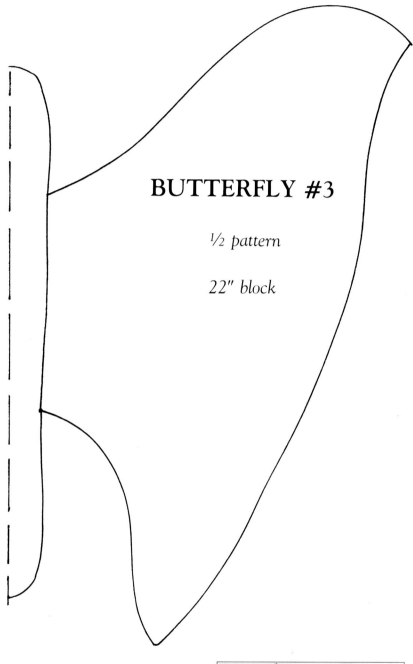

BUTTERFLY #3

½ pattern

22″ block

BUTTERFLY #4

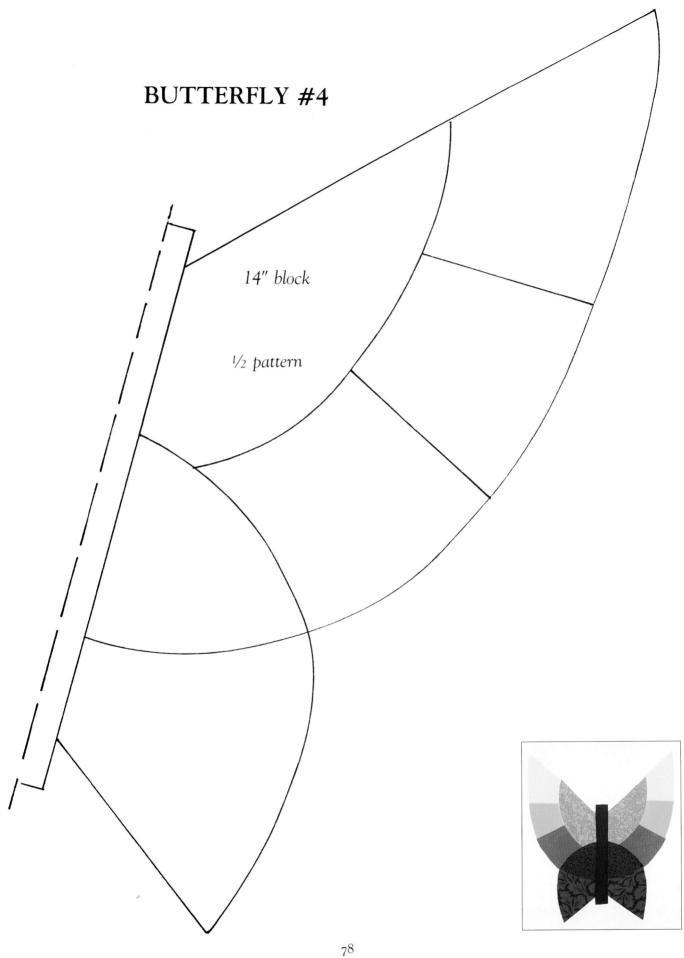

14" block

½ pattern

BUTTERFLY #5

10″ block

½ pattern

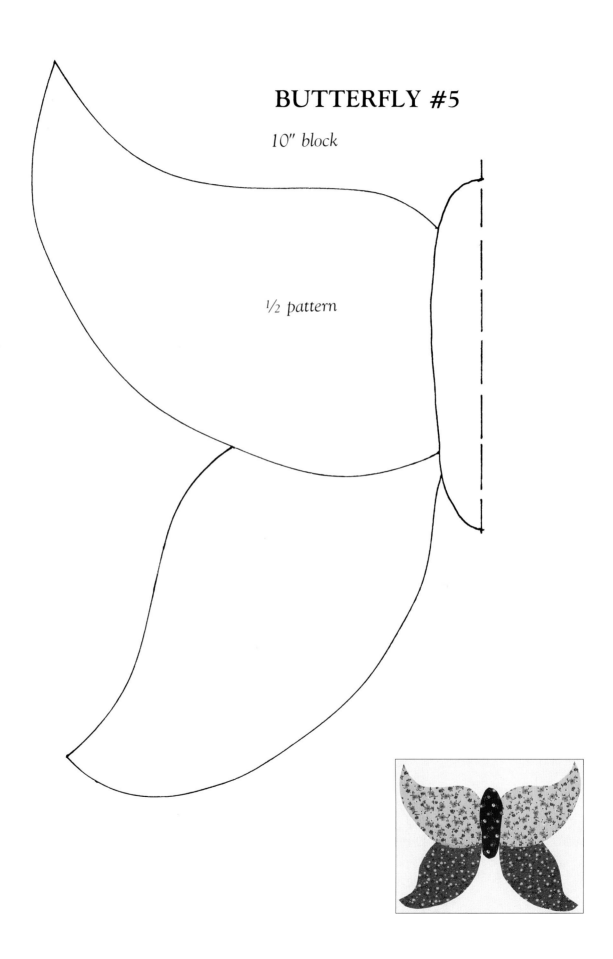

DOGWOOD

11" block

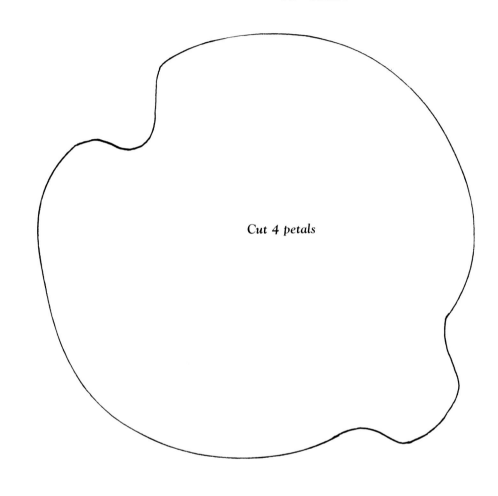

Cut 4 petals

Central circle

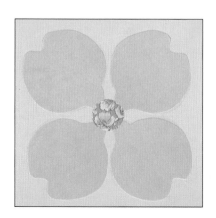

BUDS AND BLOSSOMS

9″ block

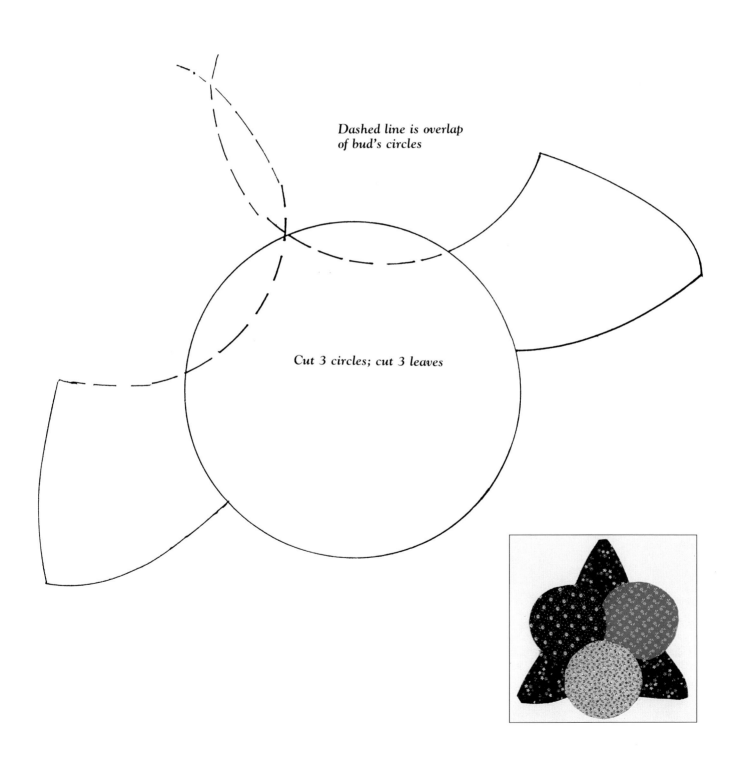

Dashed line is overlap
of bud's circles

Cut 3 circles; cut 3 leaves

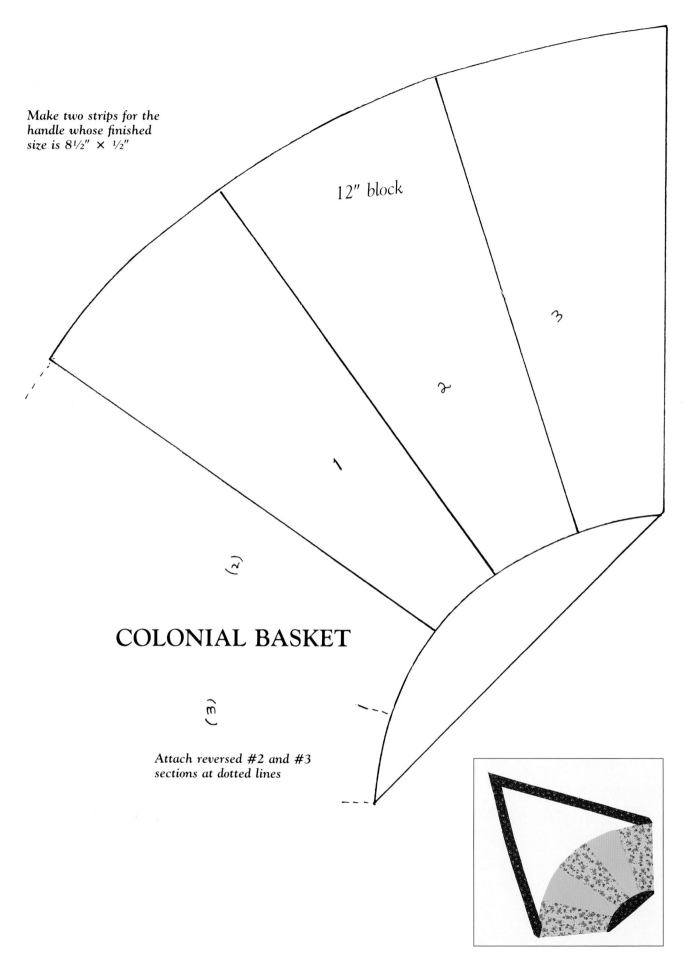

Make two strips for the handle whose finished size is 8½" × ½"

12" block

3

2

1

(2)

COLONIAL BASKET

(3)

Attach reversed #2 and #3 sections at dotted lines

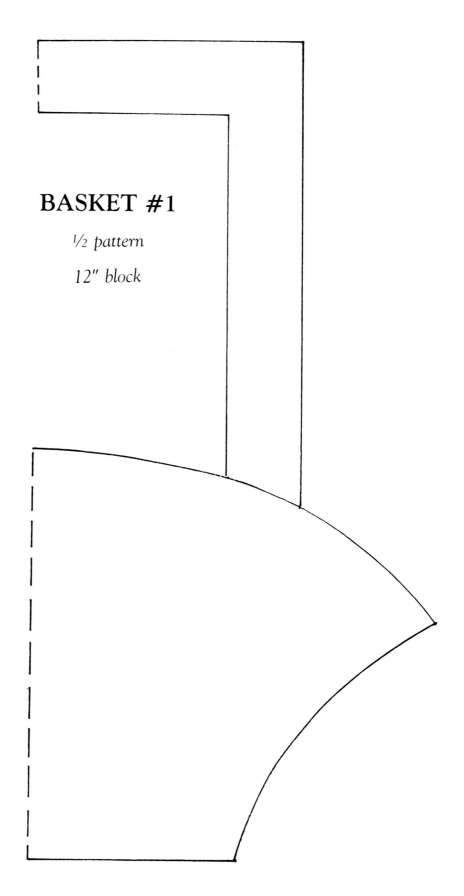

BASKET #1

½ pattern

12″ block

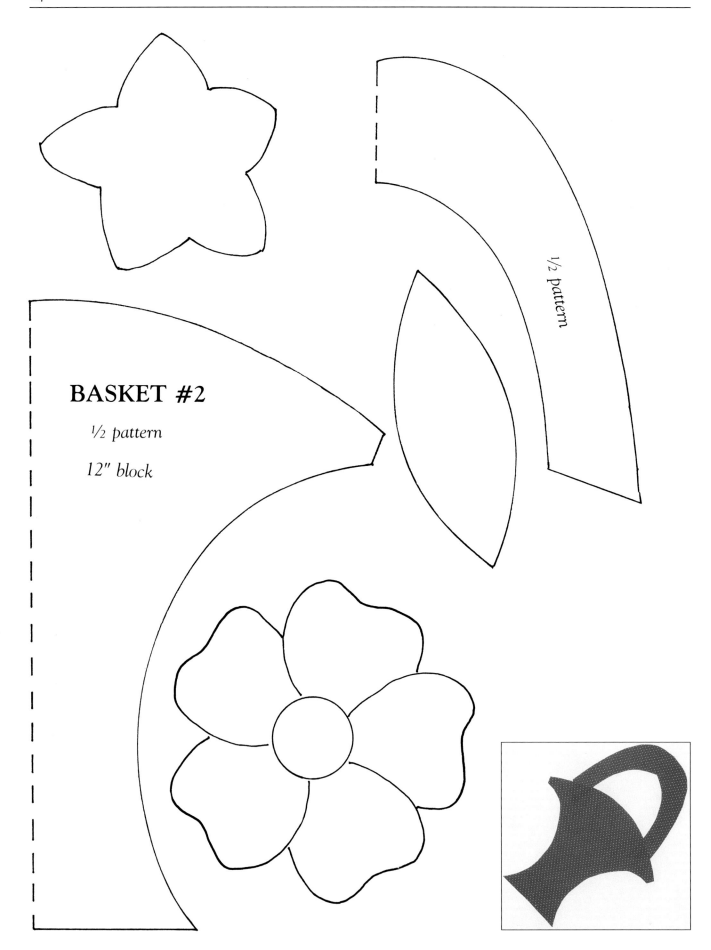

BASKET #2

½ pattern

12" block

½ pattern

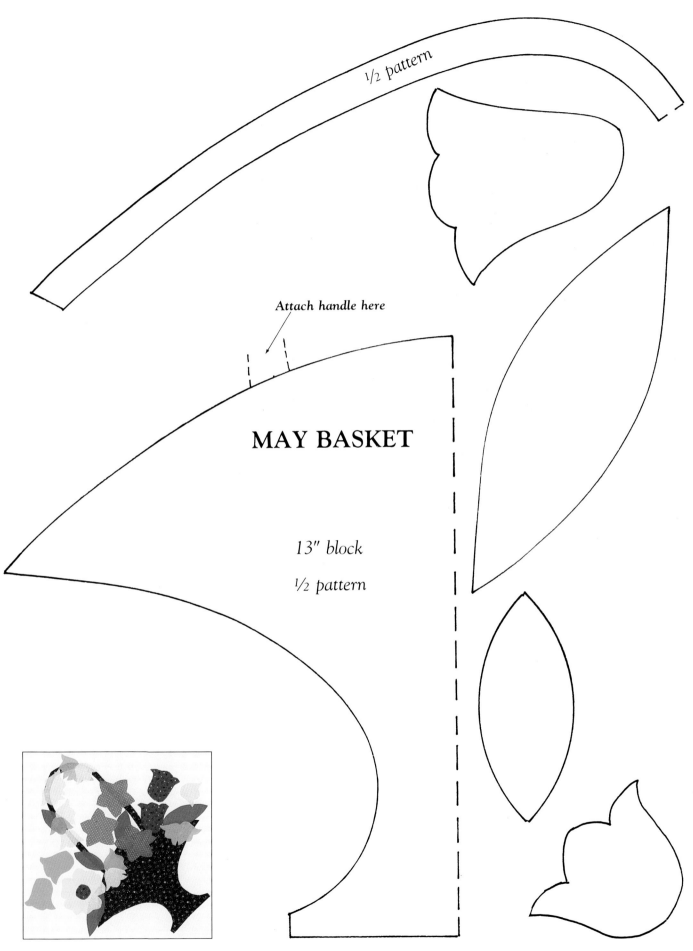

½ pattern

Attach handle here

MAY BASKET

13" block

½ pattern

CENTRAL REEL PATTERN

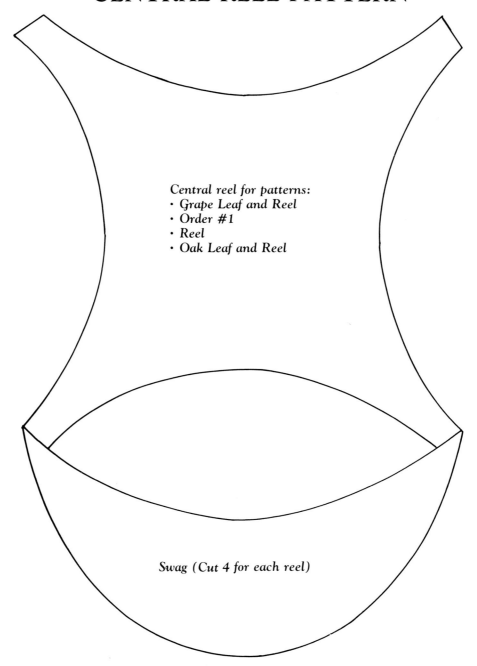

Central reel for patterns:
· Grape Leaf and Reel
· Order #1
· Reel
· Oak Leaf and Reel

Swag (Cut 4 for each reel)

GRAPE LEAF AND REEL
18" block

Central reel and
swag are on page 86.

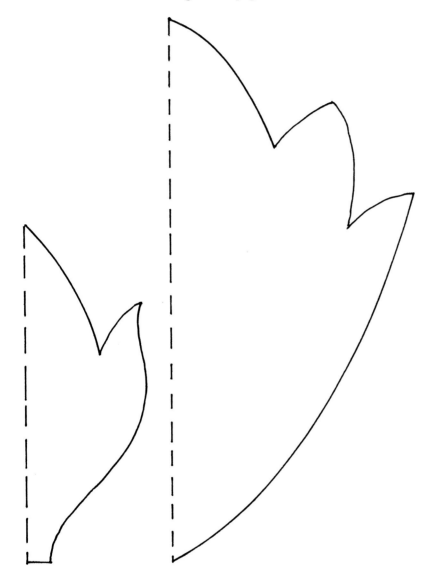

ORDER #11
12" block

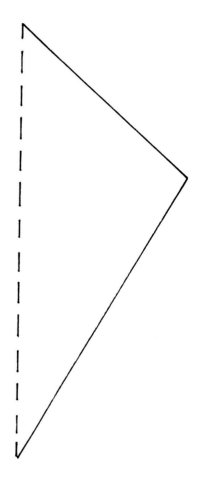

Central reel and
swag are on page 86.

OAK LEAF AND REEL

16" block

**Central reel and
swag are on page 86.**

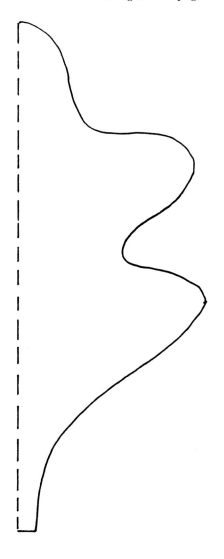

REEL

12" block

**Central reel and
swag are on page 86.**

*for reel
pattern only*

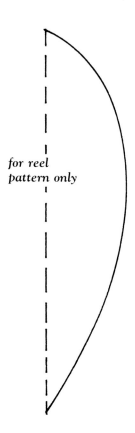

CALLIOPE
14" block

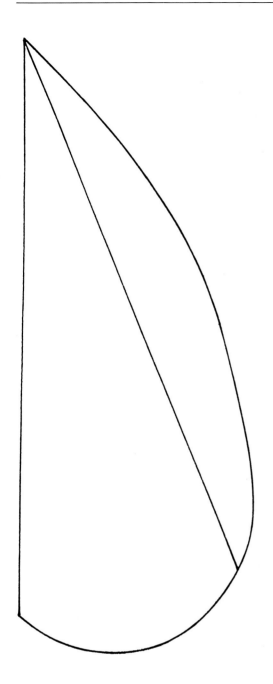

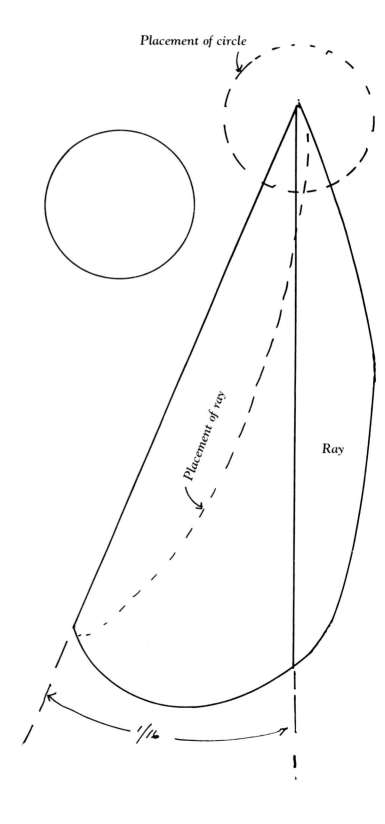

Placement of circle

Placement of ray

Ray

1/16

PINWHEEL AND OAK LEAF

16" block

Cut 16

SUNDEW

30" block

Join pattern Part 1 to Part 2 at B
to make ½ of center ray; cut 8 full rays

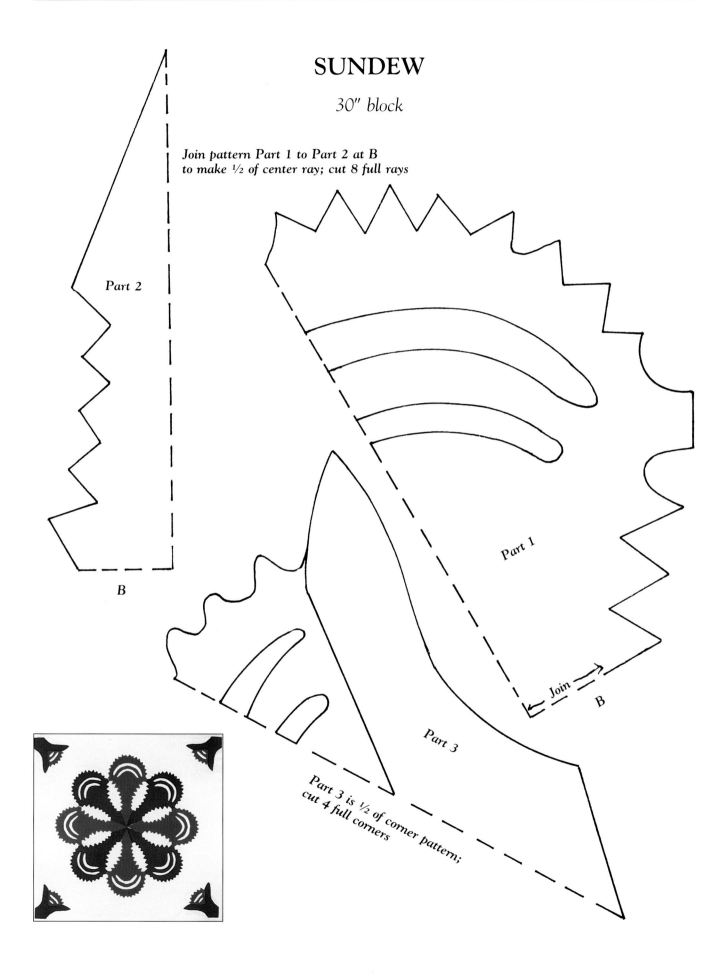

Part 2

B

Part 1

Join   B

Part 3

Part 3 is ½ of corner pattern;
cut 4 full corners

SUNDEW SWAG BORDER

For quilt border; cut as many as you need

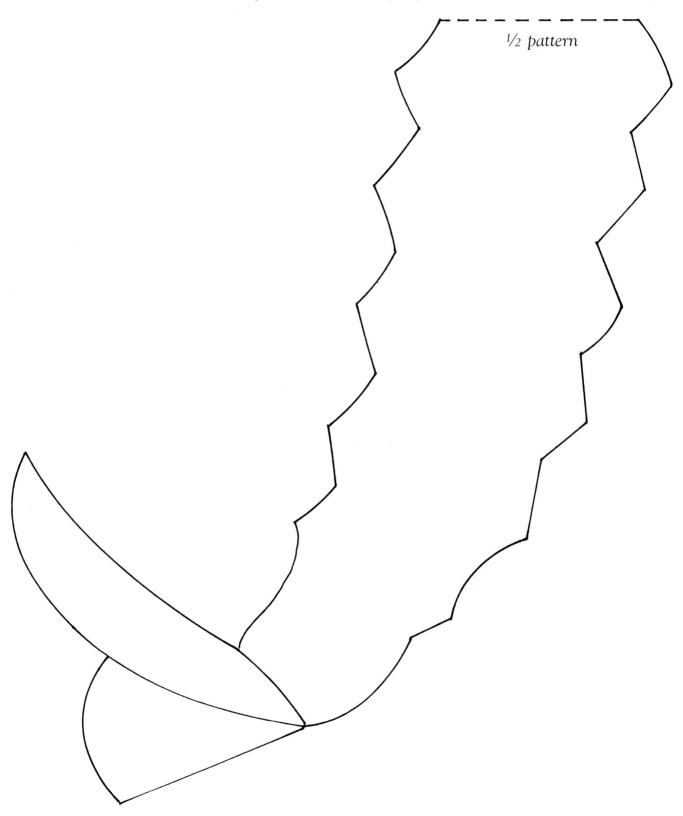

½ pattern

PRINCESS FEATHER

38" block

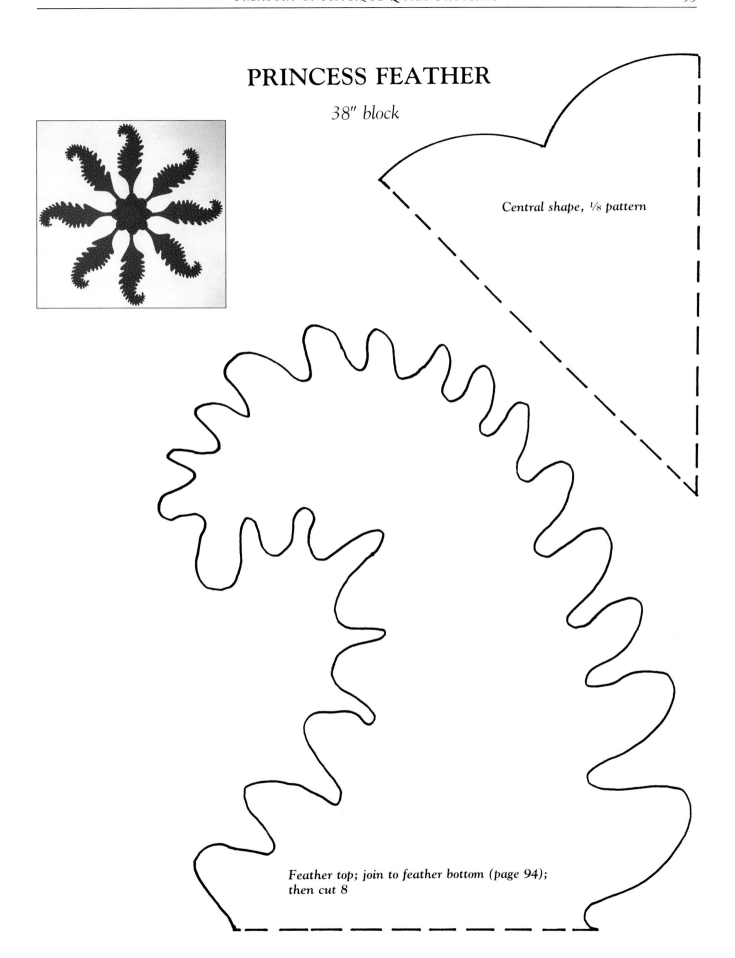

Central shape, ⅛ pattern

Feather top; join to feather bottom (page 94);
then cut 8

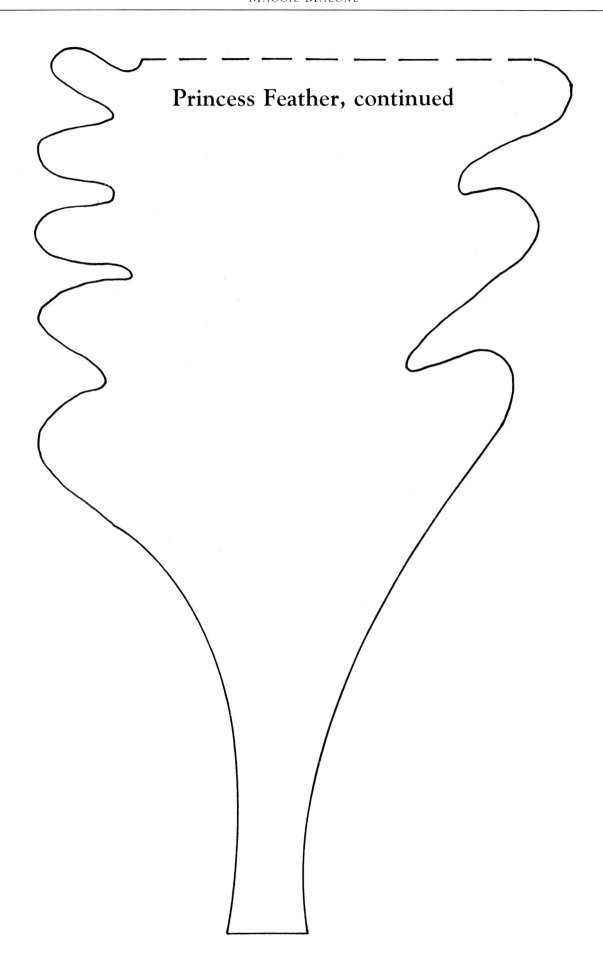

Princess Feather, continued

FLOWERS IN A POT

18" block

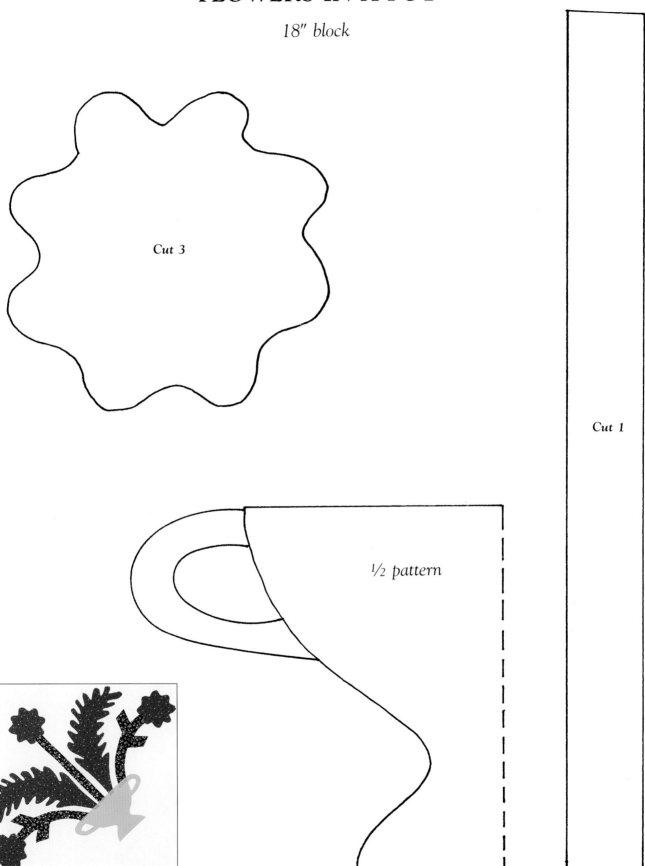

Cut 3

Cut 1

½ pattern

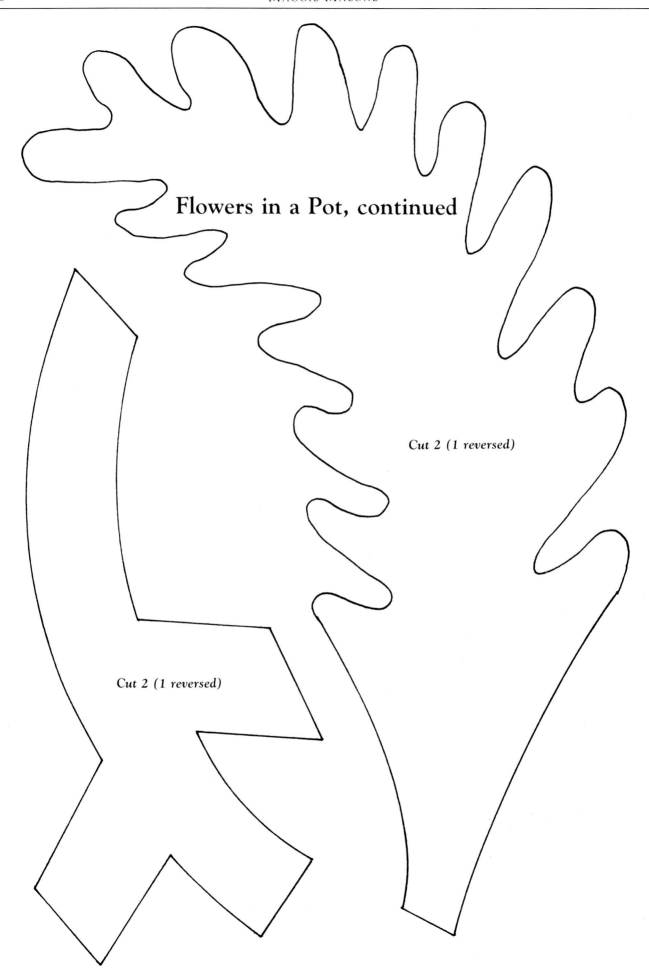

Flowers in a Pot, continued

Cut 2 (1 reversed)

Cut 2 (1 reversed)

STARS IN RED, WHITE, AND BLUE CIRCLES

16″ block

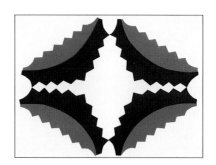

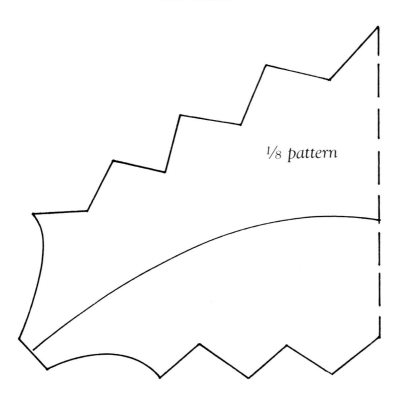

⅛ pattern

CHERRY ROSE

18″ block

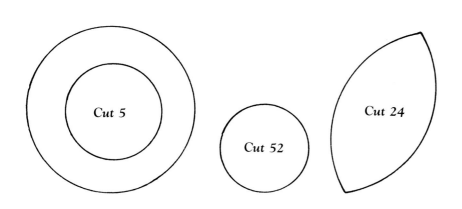

Cut 5

Cut 52

Cut 24

BOW KNOT

22" block

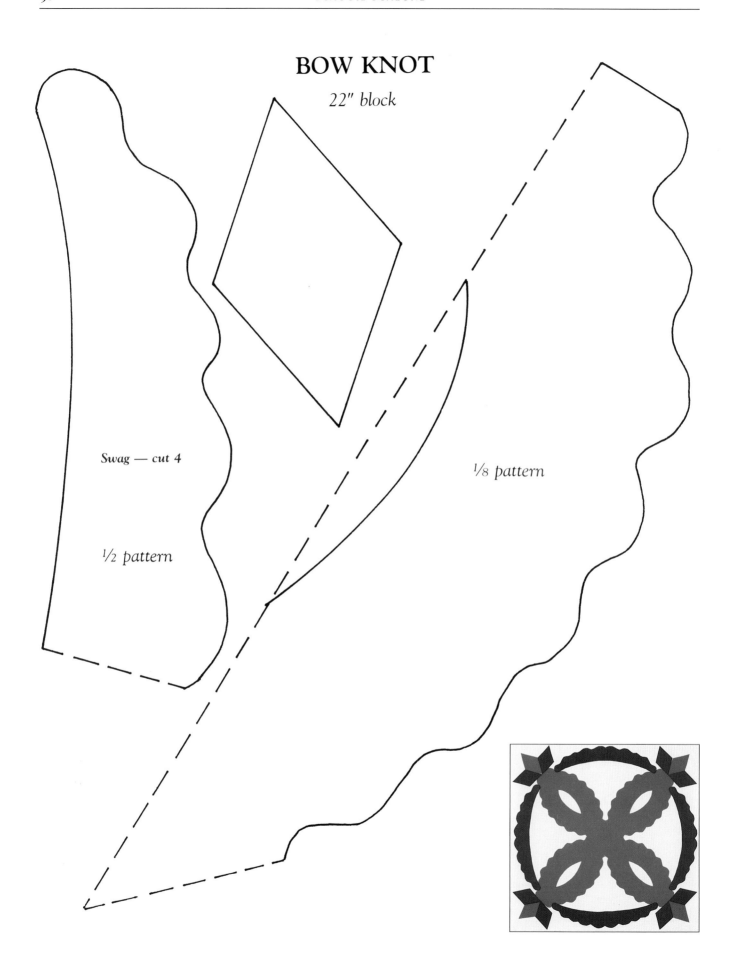

Swag — cut 4

¹⁄₂ pattern

¹⁄₈ pattern

RING AROUND THE POSY

16″ block

Outer flower

Embroider stems

Center

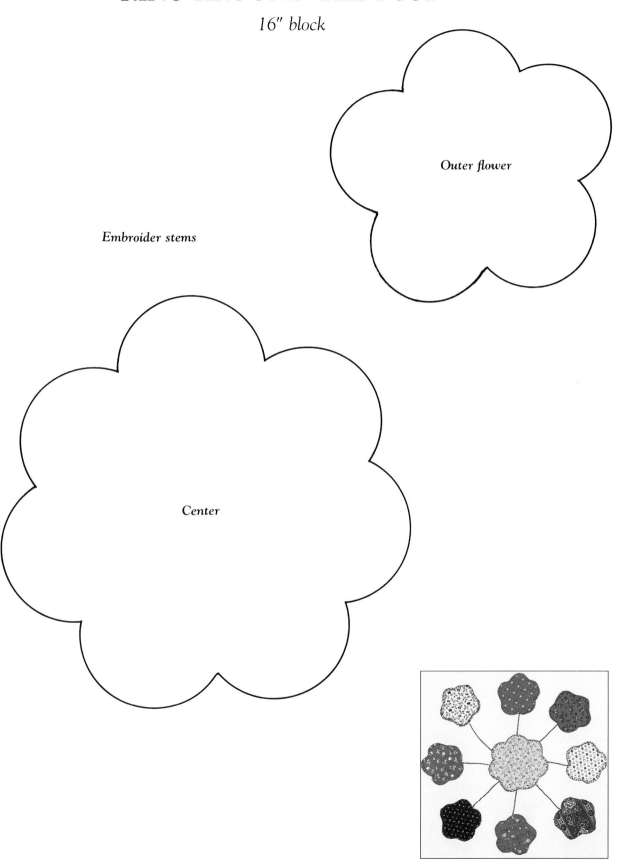

STRING OF BEADS

13″ block

ZINNIA

15″ block
¼ pattern

Cut 4 strips

Stem attached here

Stem attached here

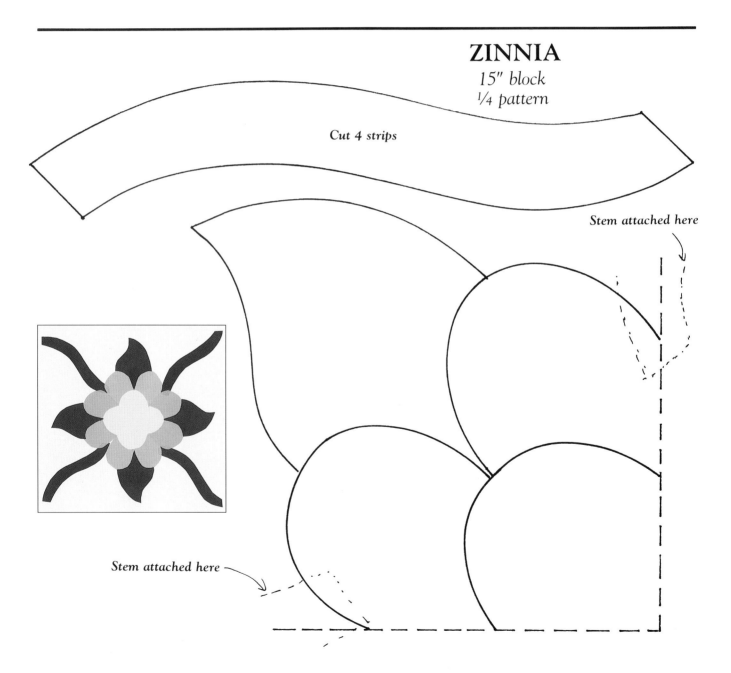

PRAIRIE FLOWER

18″ block

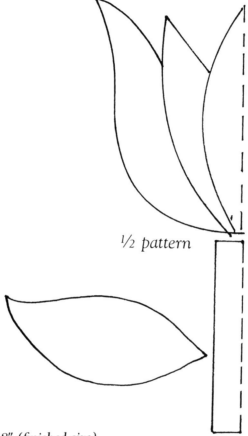

½ pattern

For stem, cut bias strip ½″ × 18″ (finished size)

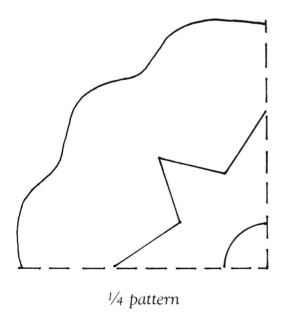

¼ pattern

ANGEL'S TRUMPET

16″ block

¹⁄₈ pattern

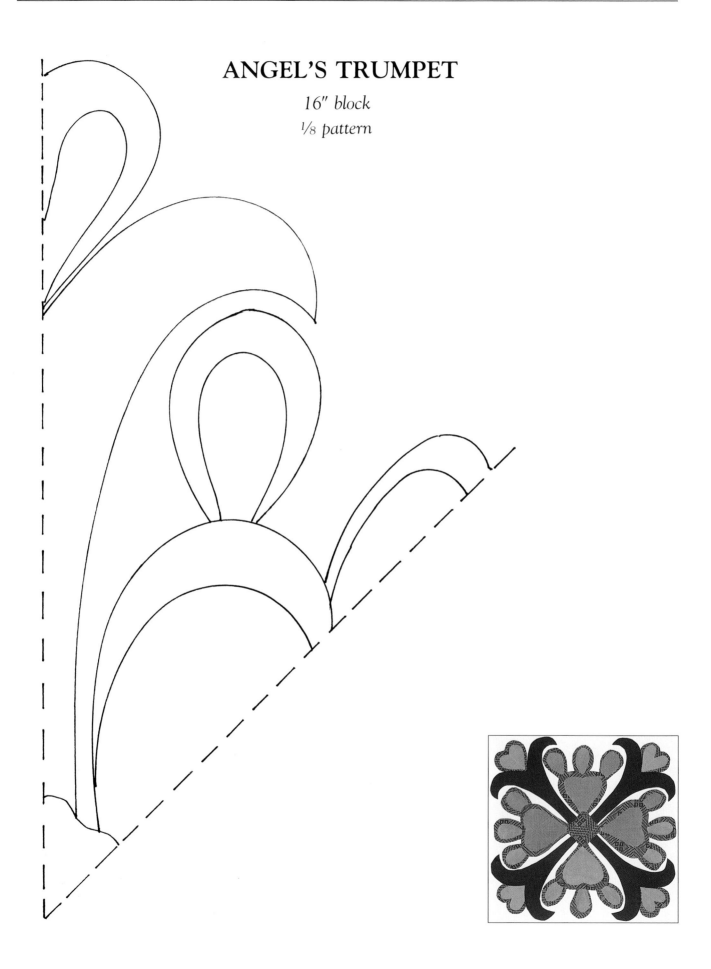

CHRISTMAS CACTUS

13" block
⅛ pattern

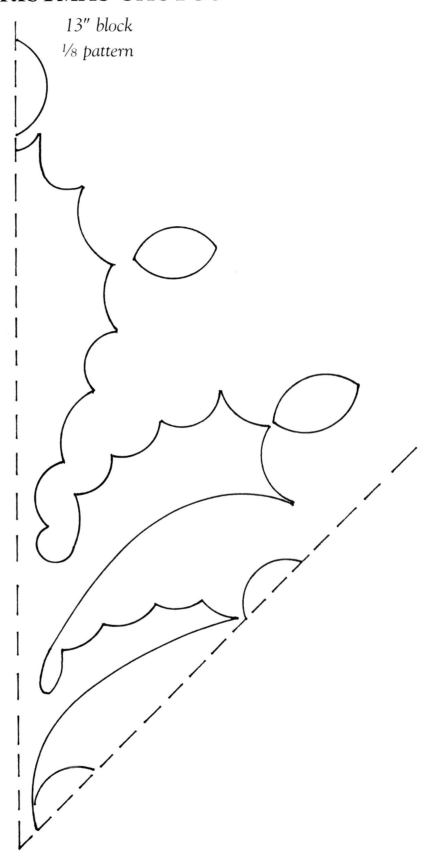

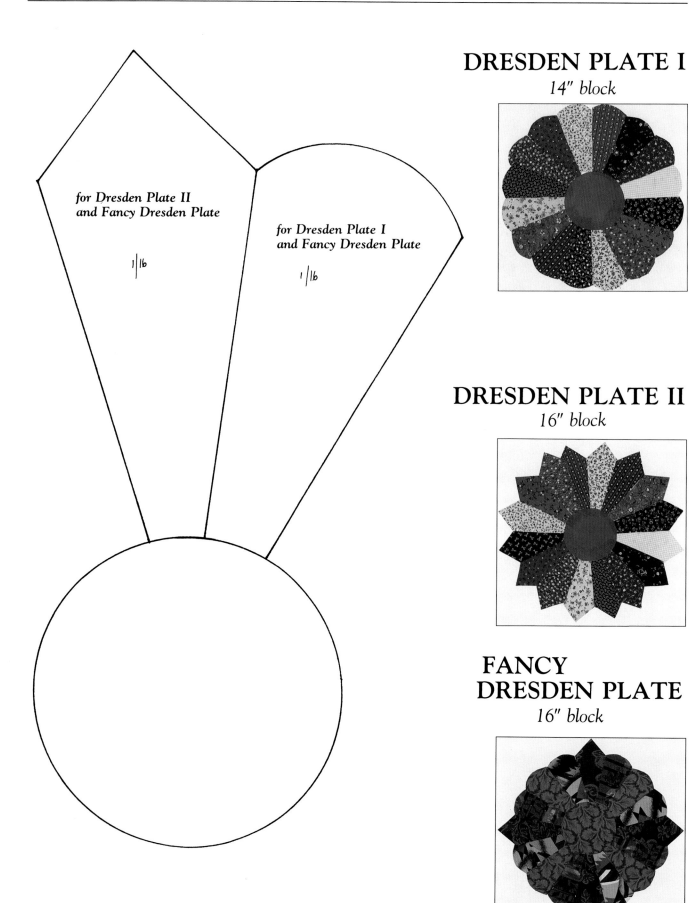

for Dresden Plate II
and Fancy Dresden Plate

1 | 16

for Dresden Plate I
and Fancy Dresden Plate

1 | 16

DRESDEN PLATE I
14" block

DRESDEN PLATE II
16" block

FANCY
DRESDEN PLATE
16" block

FRIENDSHIP DAHLIA

16″ block

⅛ pattern

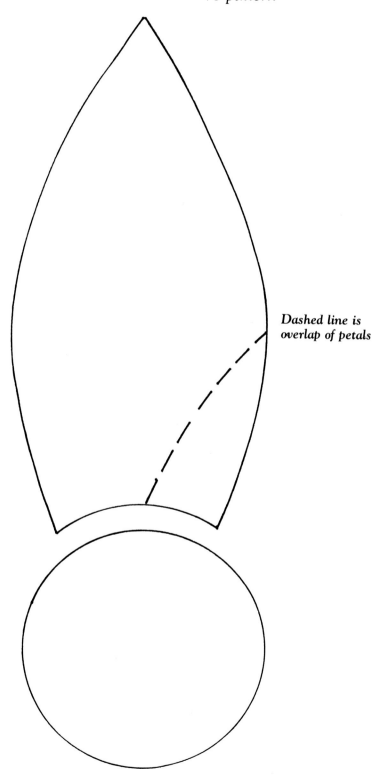

Dashed line is overlap of petals

PINEAPPLE #1

15" block

⅛ pattern

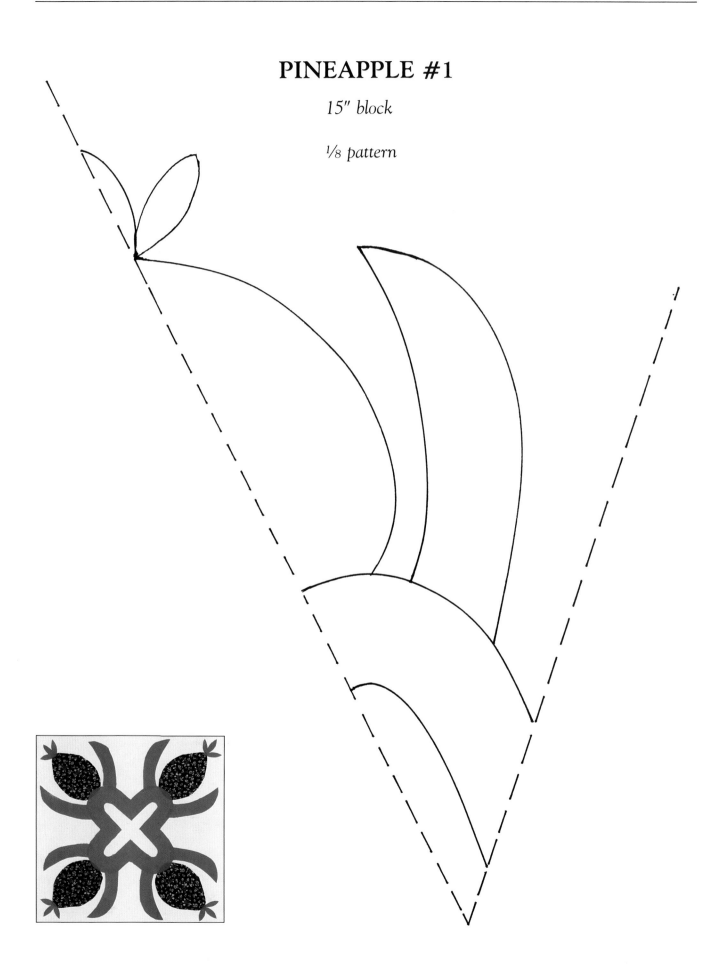

PINEAPPLE #2

16" block

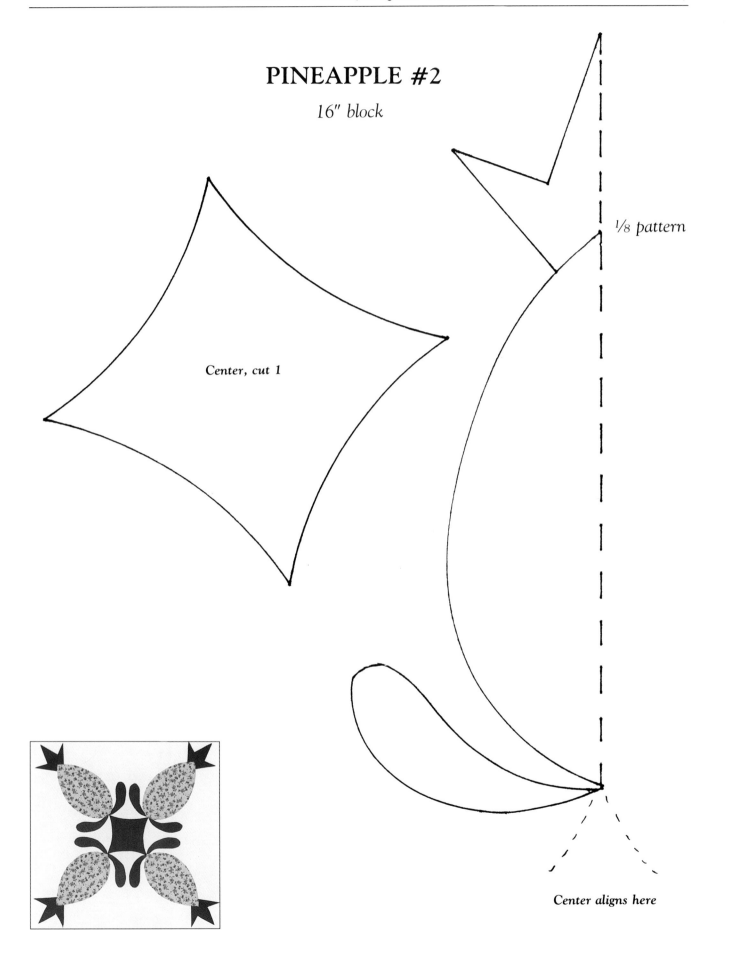

Center, cut 1

⅛ *pattern*

Center aligns here

INDIANA ROSE

12" block

⅛ pattern

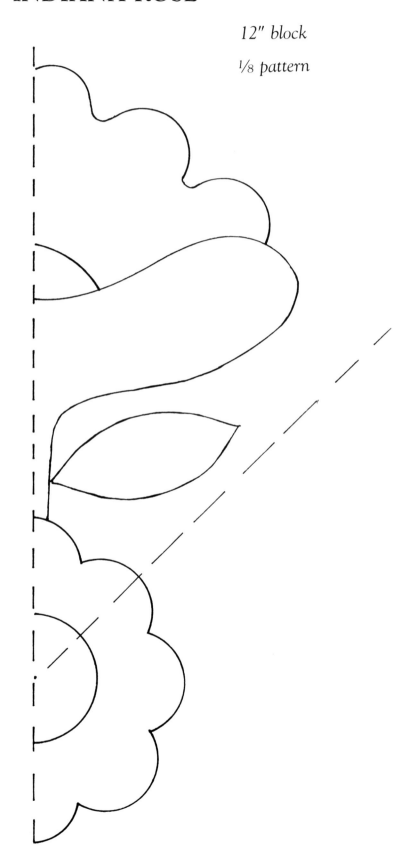

LANCASTER ROSE

14" block

¼ pattern

OHIO ROSE

15" block

⅛ pattern

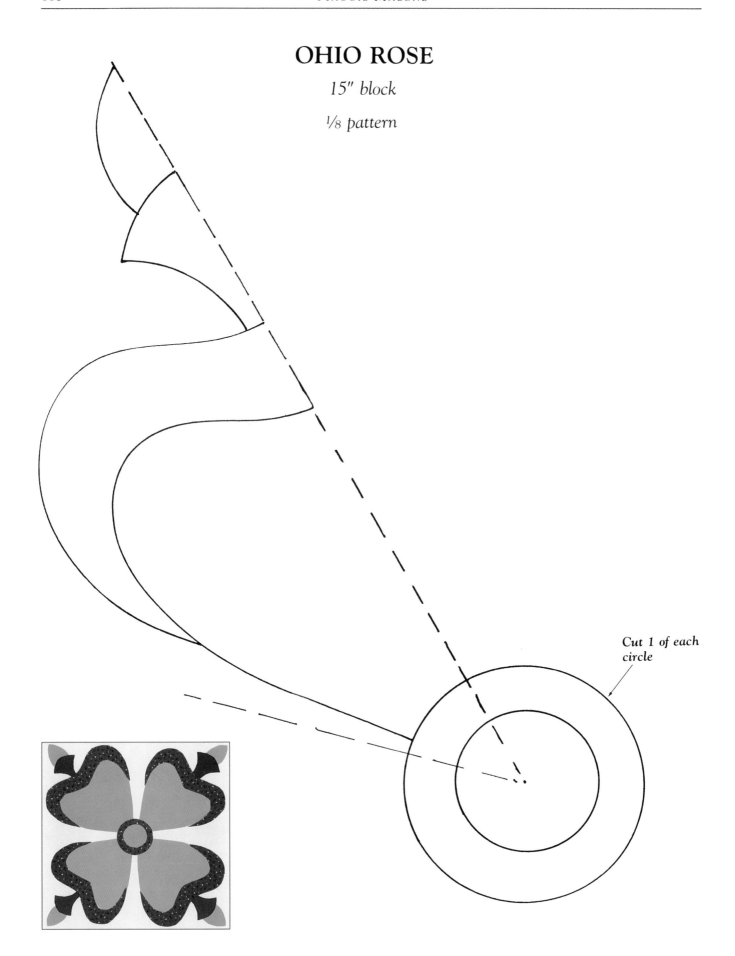

Cut 1 of each circle

ROSE CROSS

21″ block

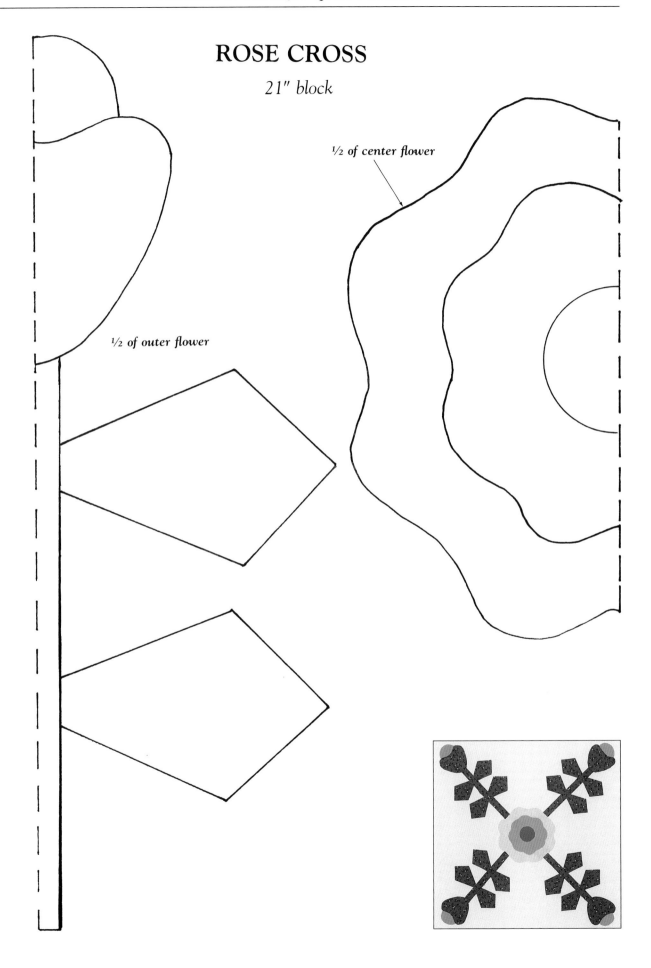

½ of center flower

½ of outer flower

OHIO ROSE BUSH

26" block

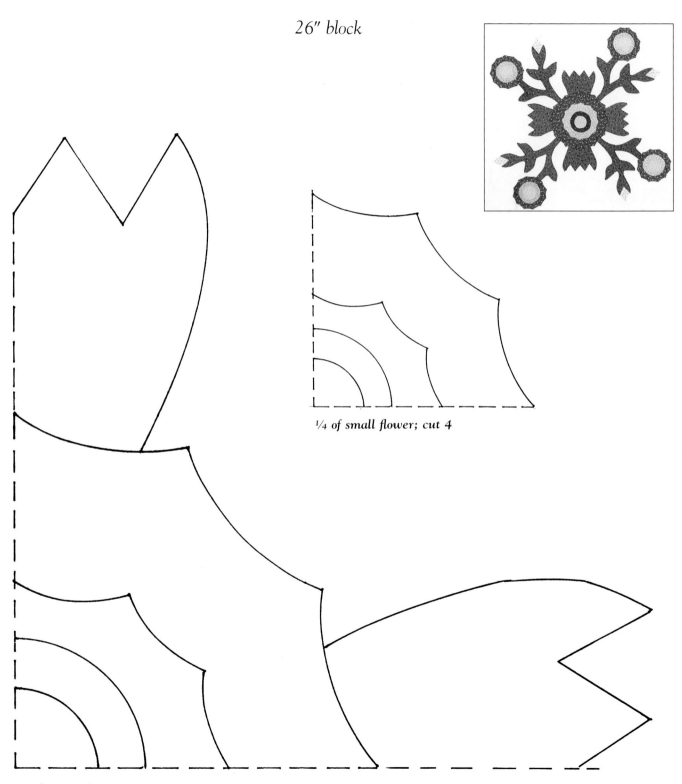

¼ *of small flower; cut 4*

¼ *of center flower*

Ohio Rose Bush, continued

Cut 4 stems

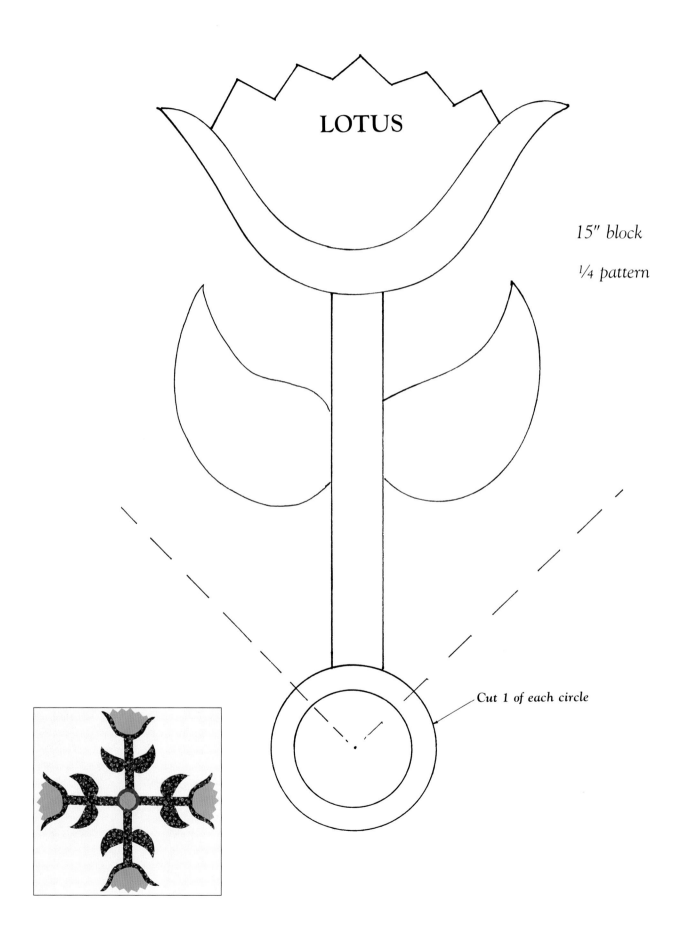

LOTUS

15″ block

¼ pattern

Cut 1 of each circle

THISTLE

14" block

⅛ pattern

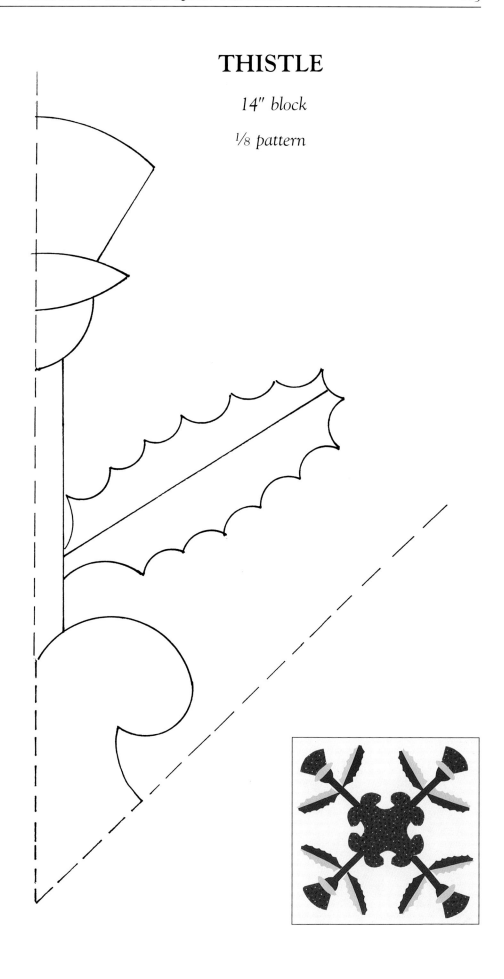

LAUREL LEAVES

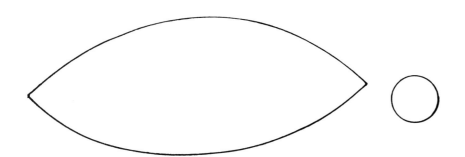

Cut 2 strips for stems, final size of each, ½″ × 12½″

CLOVER

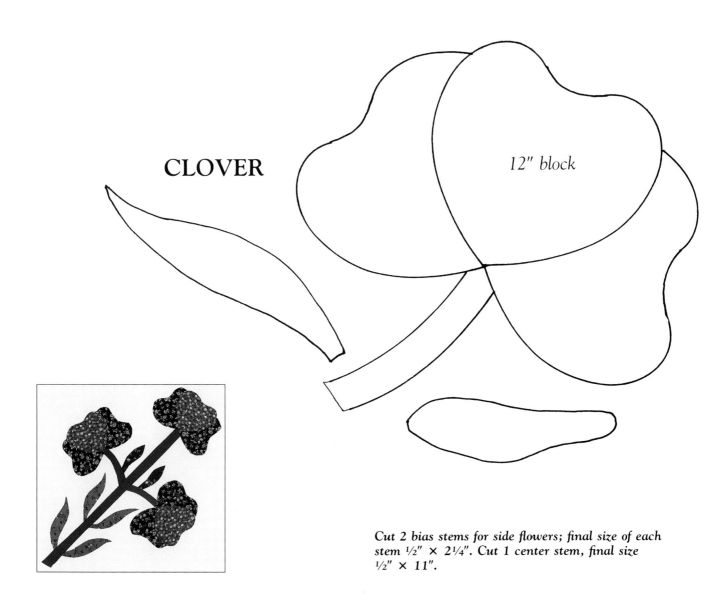

12″ block

Cut 2 bias stems for side flowers; final size of each stem ½″ × 2¼″. Cut 1 center stem, final size ½″ × 11″.

OAK LEAF AND ACORNS

18" block

Cut 4

CHERRY TREE

15" block

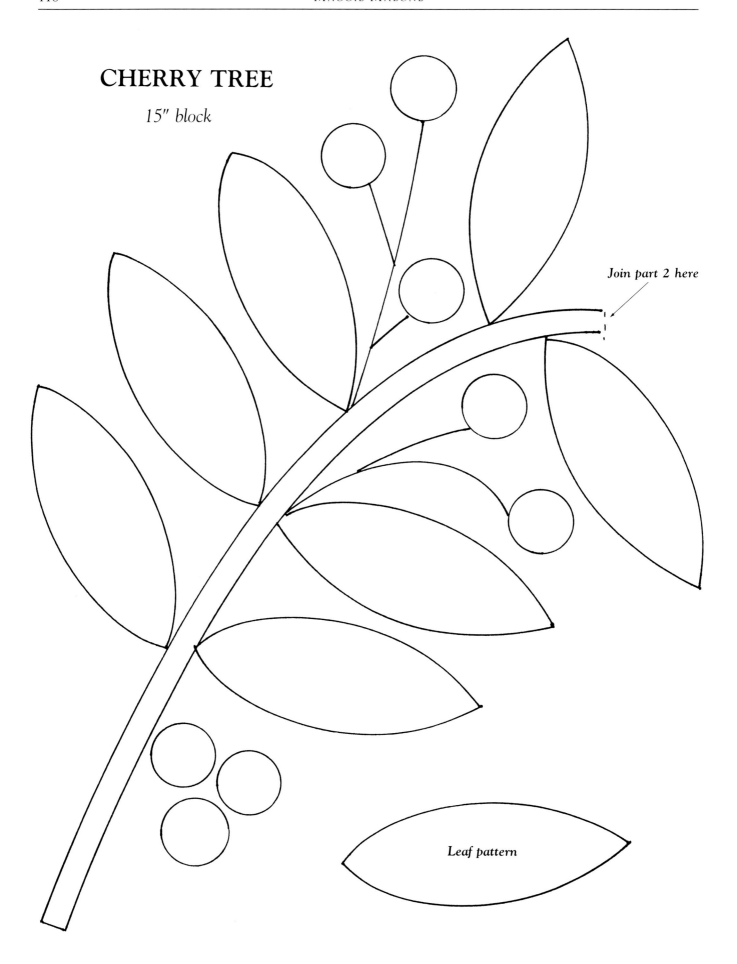

Join part 2 here

Leaf pattern

Cherry Tree, continued

WHIRLING TULIPS

14" block

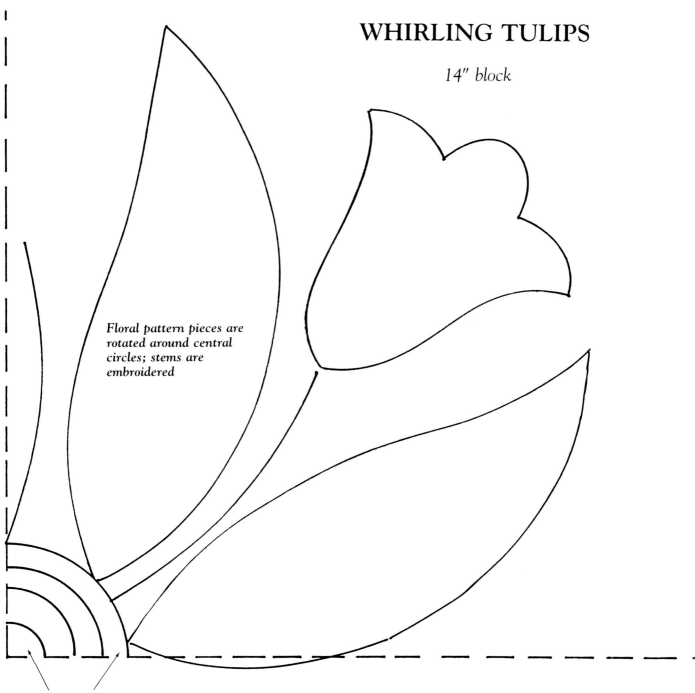

Floral pattern pieces are rotated around central circles; stems are embroidered

¼ circles pattern

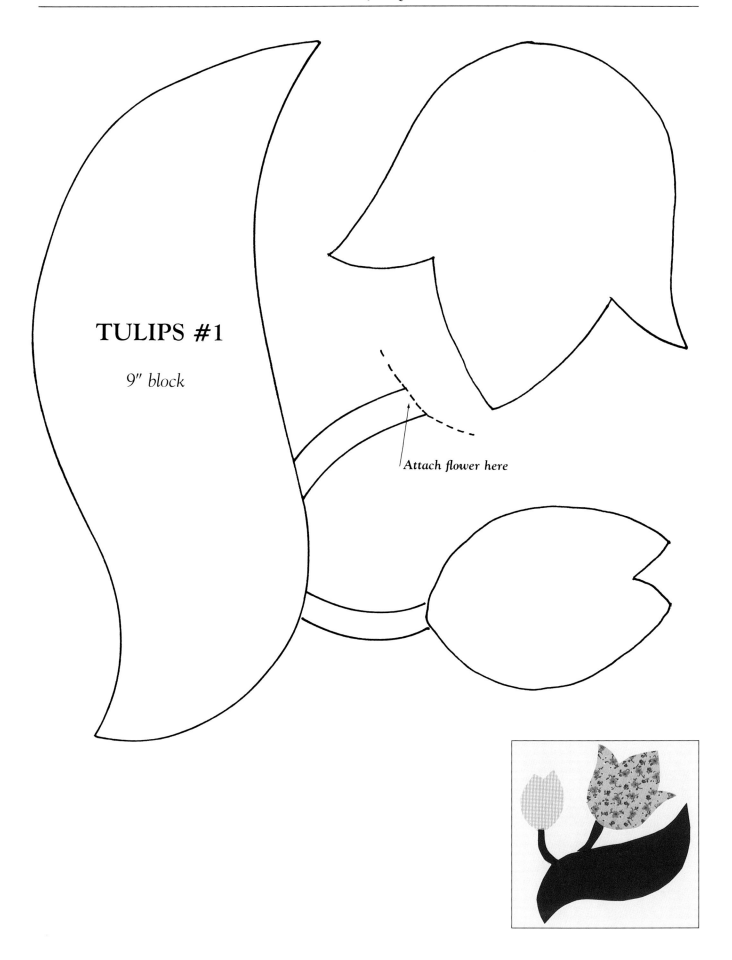

TULIPS #1

9" block

Attach flower here

TULIPS #2

16" block

½ tulip (cut 4)

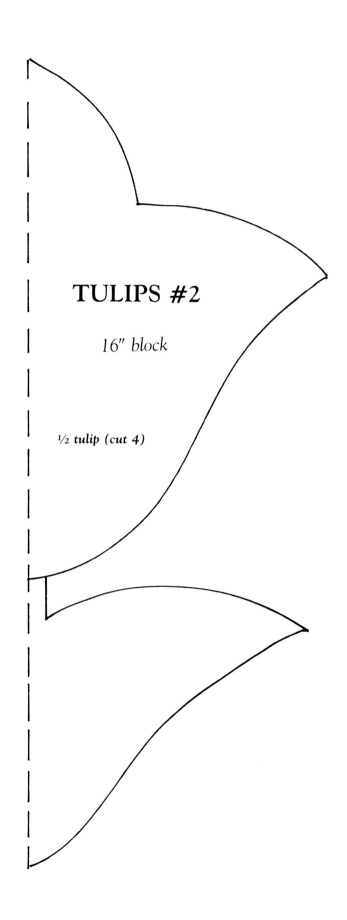

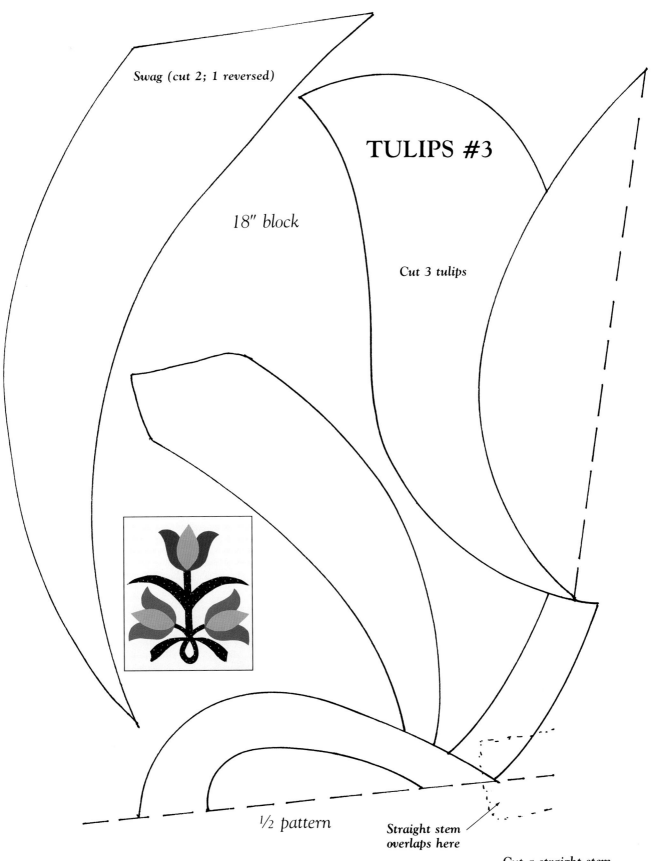

Swag (cut 2; 1 reversed)

TULIPS #3

18″ block

Cut 3 tulips

½ pattern

Straight stem
overlaps here

Cut a straight stem,
finished size of 7½″ × ⅞″
for each block.

CROSSED TULIPS #1

15" block

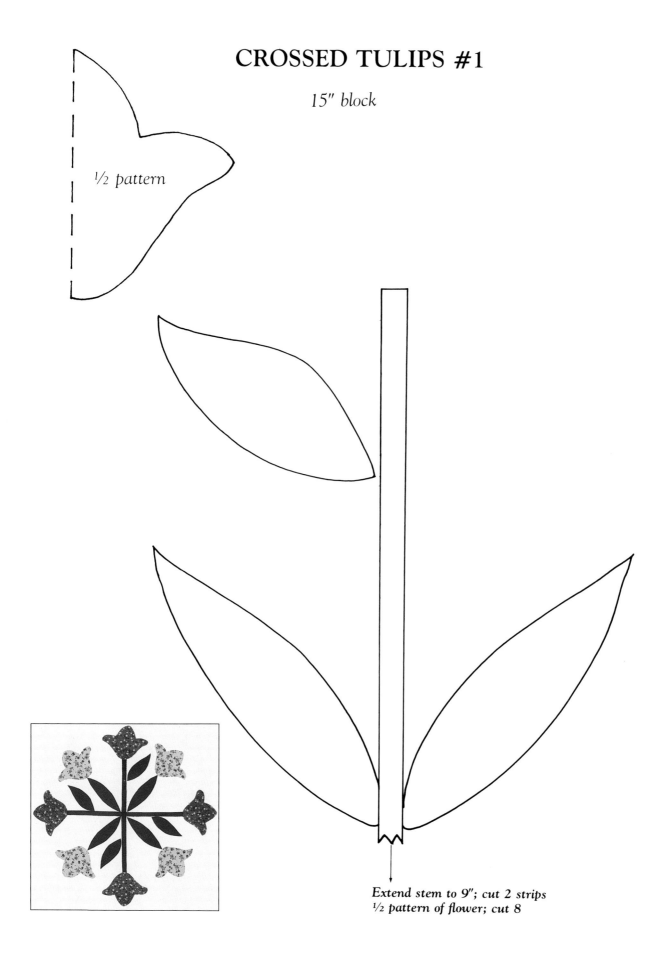

1/2 pattern

Extend stem to 9"; cut 2 strips
1/2 pattern of flower; cut 8

CROSSED TULIPS #2

22" block

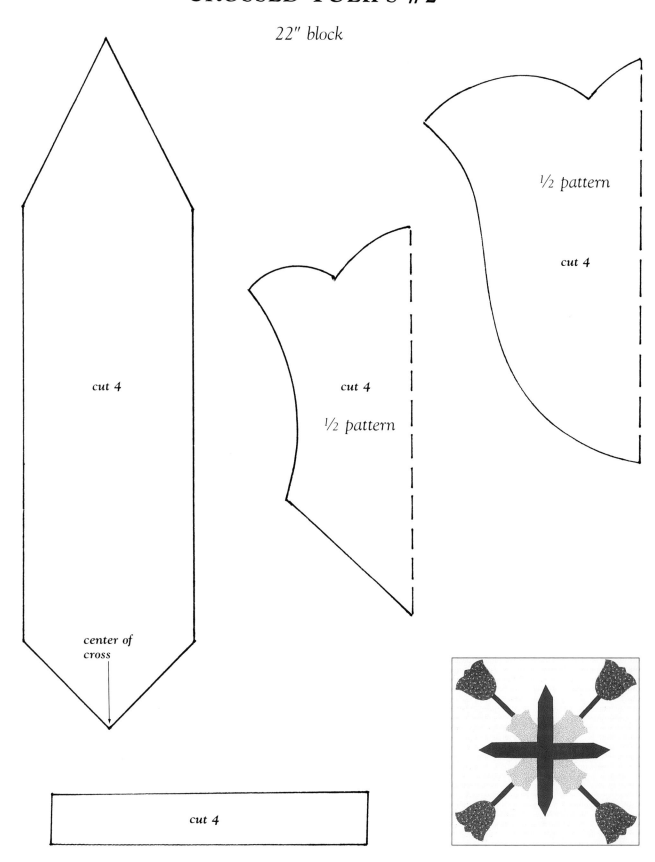

cut 4

center of
cross

½ pattern

cut 4

½ pattern

½ pattern

cut 4

cut 4

ROSE AND TULIP

18" block

HARRISON ROSE

18" block

¼ pattern

Overlap stems

SUNBONNET SUE #1

8" block

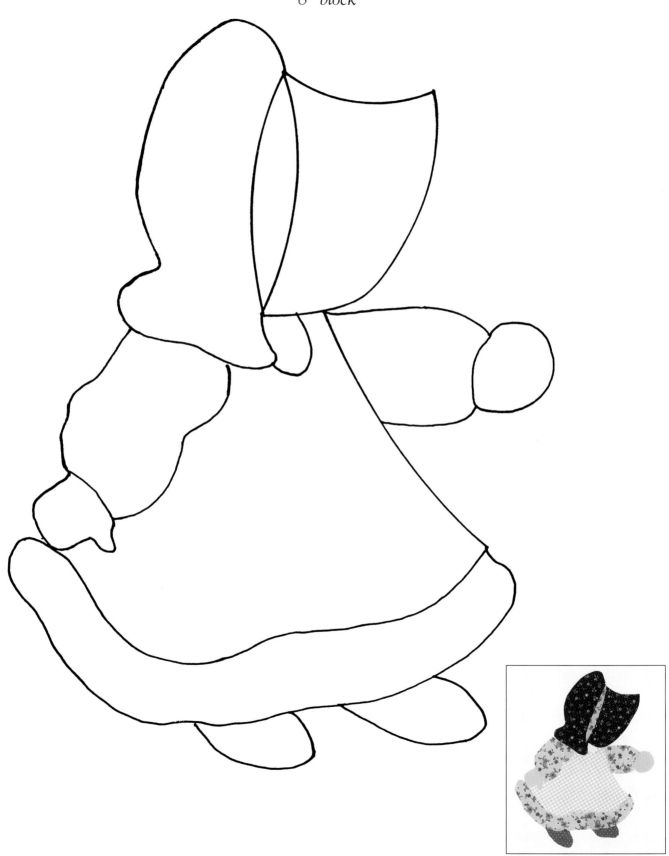

SUNBONNET SUE #2

10" block

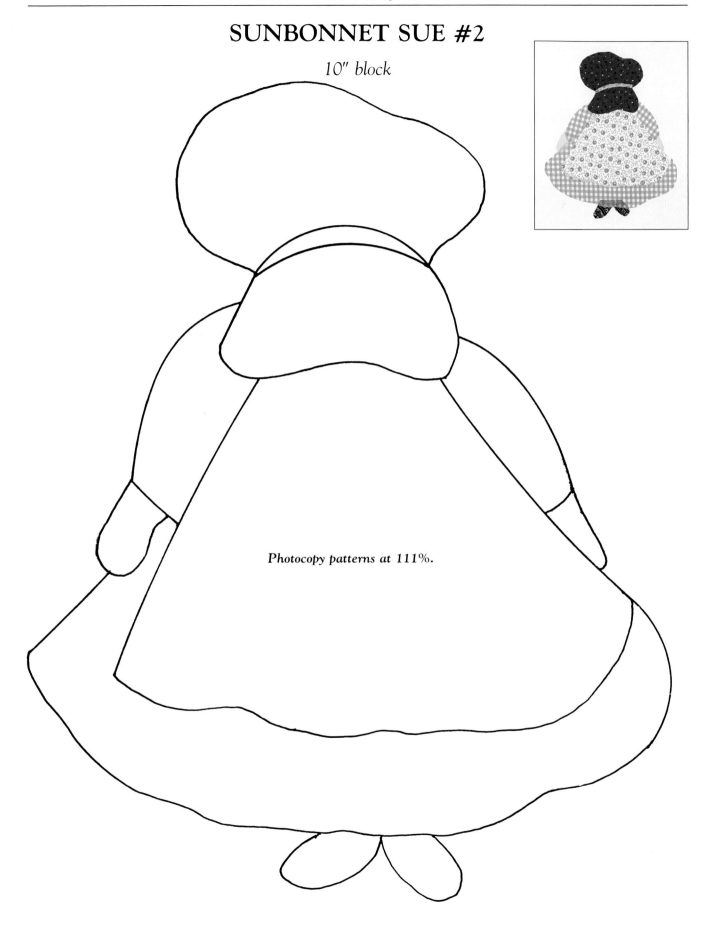

Photocopy patterns at 111%.

SUNBONNET SUE #3

12" block

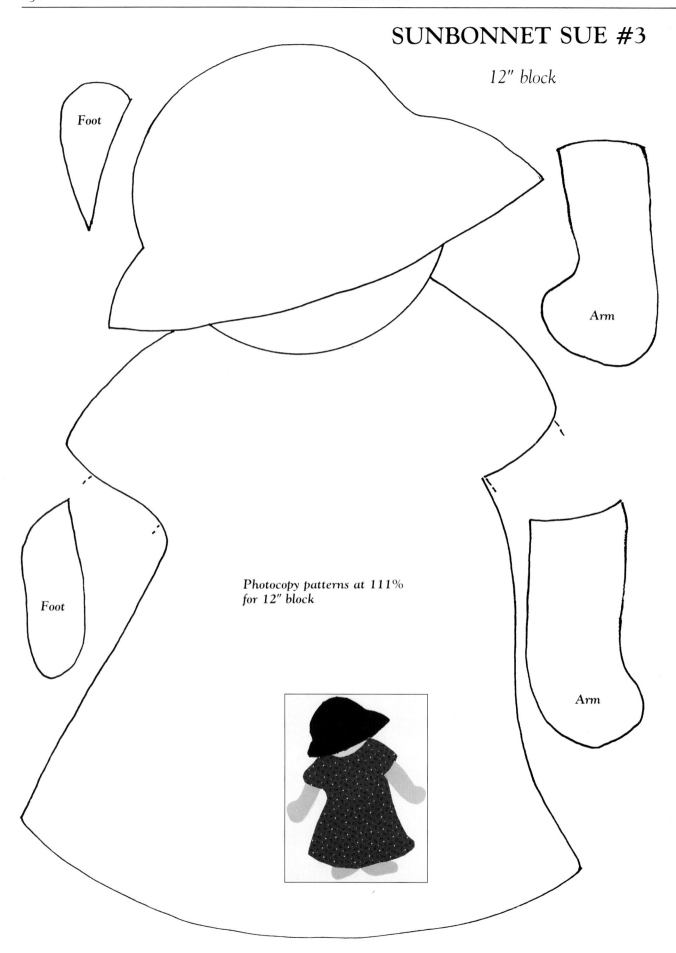

Foot

Arm

Foot

Photocopy patterns at 111%
for 12" block

Arm

OVERALL BILL #1

9" block

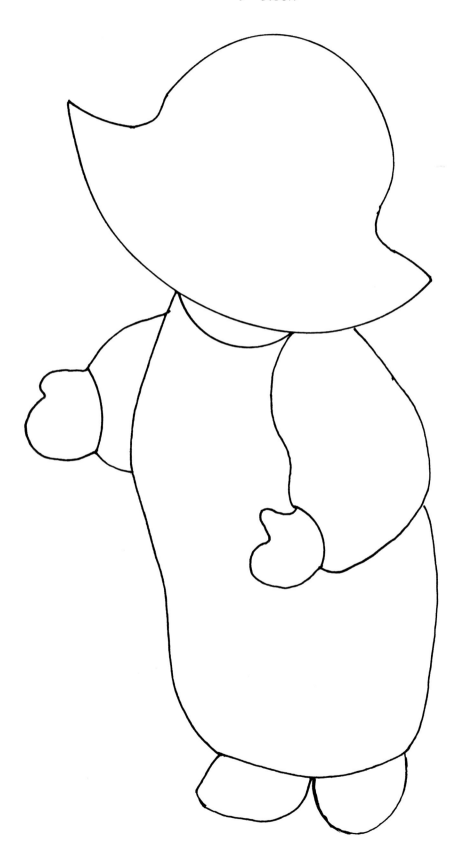

OVERALL BILL #2

10" block

OVERALL BILL #3

12" block

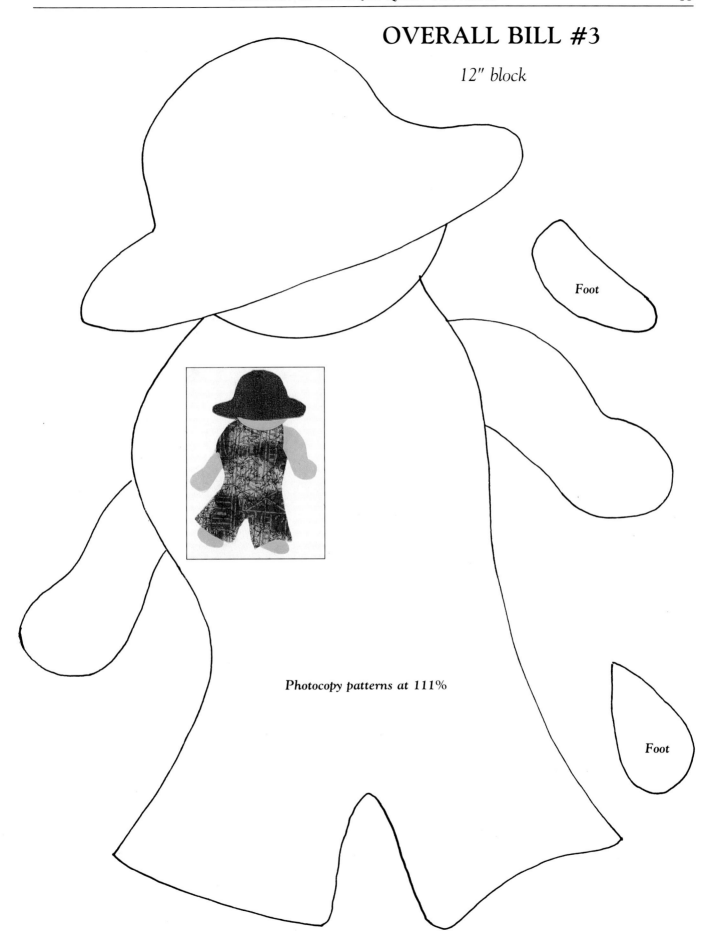

Foot

Photocopy patterns at 111%

Foot

POMEGRANATE BLOCK

¼ pattern

18″ block

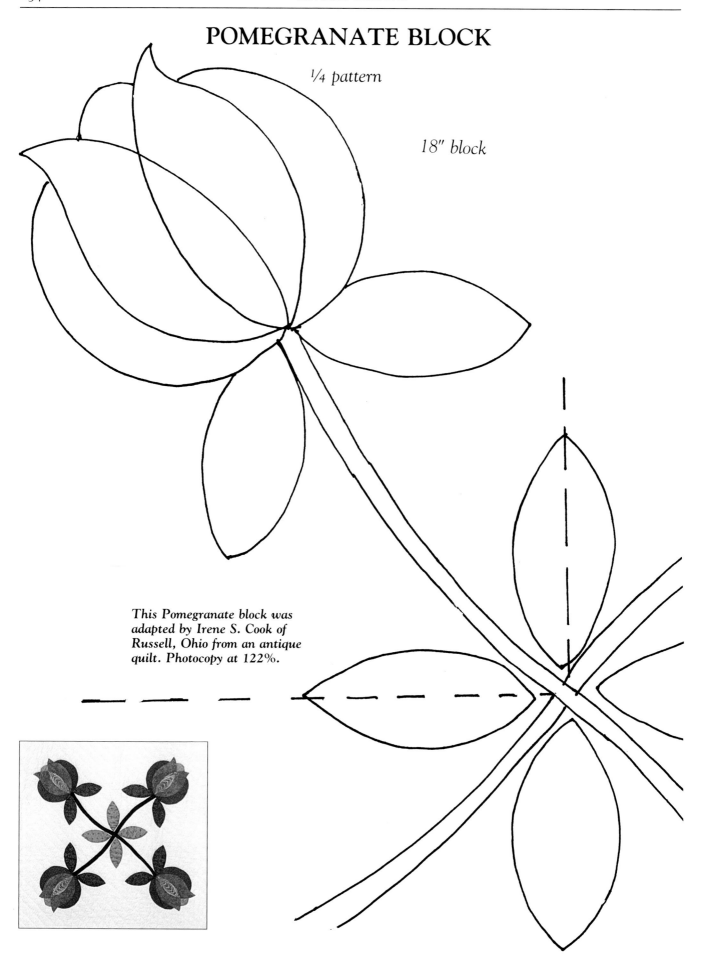

This Pomegranate block was adapted by Irene S. Cook of Russell, Ohio from an antique quilt. Photocopy at 122%.

KENTUCKY PRINCESS FEATHER

18" block

¼ pattern

This Princess Feather pattern was published by the Kentucky Heritage Society of Lexington, Kentucky in the Kentucky Medallion Appliqué Book in 1984. Photocopy at 117%

WREATH AND BUILDING

overlap
pattern halves
here

96 + 97
Terminal on
Gray

NOTES: R = red
g = green
y = yellow
bl = blue

✻ : Reverse appliqué
P = pink

This Wreath and Building Pattern was designed by Cheryl Pedersen of Novelty, Ohio, in 1991 for her Baltimore Sampler Quilt. Photocopy at 154%. Overlap pattern halves (pages 136 and 137) on the dashed lines.

TERMINAL TOWER

CHRYSANTHEMUM
9" block

This is Irene Goodrich's version of Ruby S. McKim's Chrysanthemum pattern, at 114%
the original pattern size. Piece numbering by Irene Goodrich.

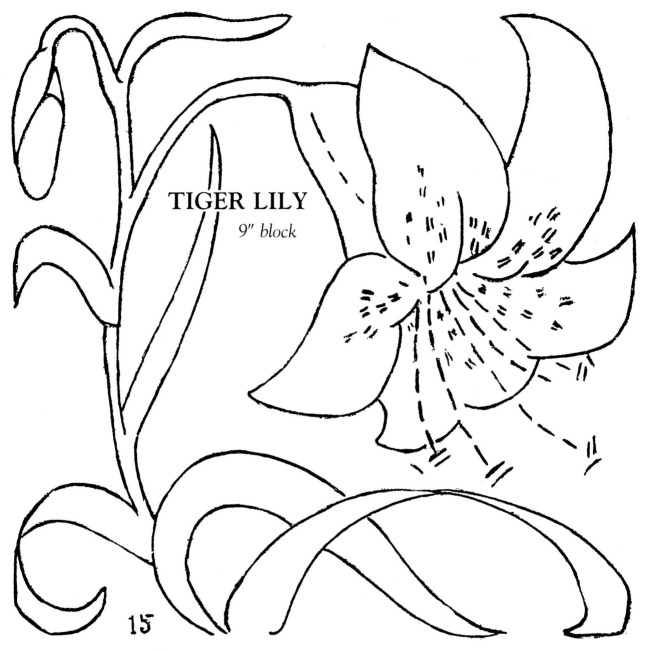

TIGER LILY

9" block

15

This Ruby Short McKim pattern originally appeared in the State Journal of Columbus, Ohio, in 1930. Irene Goodrich used it at the size shown here (114% of the original).

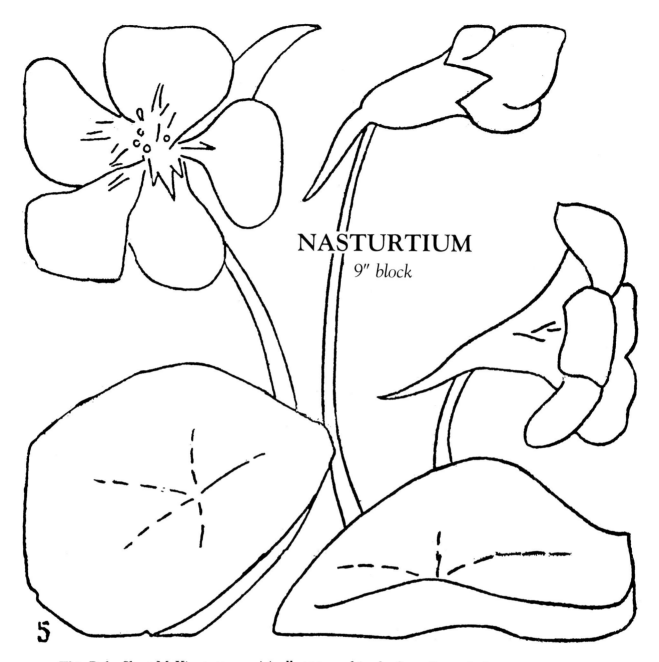

NASTURTIUM
9" block

5

This Ruby Short McKim pattern originally appeared in the State Journal of Columbus, Ohio, in 1930. Irene Goodrich used it at the size shown here (114% of the original).

BLEEDING HEART

9″ block

This *Ruby Short McKim pattern originally appeared in the State Journal of Columbus, Ohio, in 1930. Irene Goodrich used it at the size shown here (114% of the original).*

PERMISSIONS AND PHOTO CREDITS

Note: unless otherwise noted, all quilts shown in the book are under copyright of their creators and reprinted here by permission, and by permission of the photographers.

Noah's Ark was hand appliquéd by Peggy Deierhoi, machine quilted by Nancy Watts from 1992–1993. Front of quilt pattern from *Noah,* by Red Wagon, Liberty, Missouri. Back of quilt pattern by Peggy Deierhoi. Photographed by Larry London (page 31).

Creatures of the Night was designed, appliquéd and quilted in 1992 by Nola Eschedor, Akron, Ohio. Photographed by David Thum (page 37); closeup photos by Isabel Stein (pages 24, 37). Reproduced by permission.

Barnyard was designed, appliquéd, and quilted in 1994 by Nola Eschedor, Akron, Ohio. Photographed by David Thum, Lakewood, Ohio (page 40).

Royal Cross was appliquéd and quilted by Anne Doherty, Akron, Ohio, in 1990 from a kit by Judie Rothermel, Schoolhouse Designs, Canton, Ohio. Photographed by David Thum (page 6).

Thunderbird, appliquéd and quilted by Anne Doherty, of Akron, Ohio, is based on an old Pueblo Indian design; pattern made by Fran Soika, of Novelty, Ohio. Photograph by Anne Doherty (page 29).

Ruby S. McKim Flower Garden, a prize-winning quilt, was appliquéd and quilted by Irene Goodrich, Columbus, Ohio, in 1977 from patterns by Ruby Short McKim that originally appeared in the *Ohio State Journal* newspaper in the 1930s. Full quilt photographed by Larry London (page 43). Closeups photographed by Isabel Stein (pages 43, 63, 64).

Moss Ross was appliquéd and quilted by Irene Goodrich, Columbus, Ohio, in 1988 from patterns by Nancy Cabot that appeared in the *Chicago Tribune* in the 1930s, 1940s, and 1950s. Photographed by Larry London (page 42).

Exteriors #1, designed, appliquéd, and quilted by Clare M. Murray, Canton, Ohio in 1990. Photographed by Clare M. Murray (page 35).

Exteriors #3, designed, appliquéd and quilted by Clare M. Murray, 1990, Canton, Ohio. Photographed by Clare M. Murray (page 34).

Interior #3, designed, appliquéd and quilted by Clare M. Murray in 1993. Photograph by Jeff Collier (page 34).

Victorian Ladies, designed, appliquéd, and quilted by Betty Nye of Columbus, Ohio, in 1980. Closeup photographs by Betty Nye (pages 29, 36); full quilt photograph by David Thum (page 36).

Heirloom Appliqué, appliquéd and quilted by Betty Nye of Columbus, Ohio from a pattern in Pat Andreatta's book, *Heirloom Appliqué.* Photograph by Larry London (page 41). Reproduced by permission of Pat Andreatta.

Baltimore Sampler Quilt, designed, appliquéd and quilted by Cheryl Pedersen of Novelty, Ohio, in 1991, includes her own original appliqué patterns as well as the Princess Feather block (pages 63, 135), from the *Kentucky Medallion Appliqué Book,* published by the Kentucky Heritage Quilt Society of Lexington, Kentucky, in 1984, reprinted by permission. The Wreath and Terminal Tower Building block (pages 63, 136–137) is an original appliqué pattern by Cheryl Pedersen. The Pomegranate Block (pages 63, 134) was adapted by Irene S. Cook of Russell, Ohio, from an antique quilt design. The full quilt (page 42) was photographed by Larry London. Closeups (pages 42, 63) photographed by Isabel Stein. The Rose Wreath on page 28 is from Rita Woloshuk's *Baltimore Bride's Quilt Pattern Book,* from Rita's Quilt & Sewing Center, Albuquerque, N.M.

Frog on a Lily Pad was designed, appliquéd, and quilted by Linda Smith Poole of Mentor, Ohio, in 1991. Photographed by Isabel Stein (page 30).

Peony was appliquéd and quilted by Linda Smith Poole of Mentor, Ohio, in 1982 from a traditional design. Photographed by Larry London (page 44).

Frogmoor and the Blue Moose was designed, quilted, and appliquéd by Linda Smith Poole of Mentor, Ohio, in 1992. Photographed by Larry London (page 39).

Miniature Hanover Tulip, appliquéd and quilted by Leita E. Shahan of Geneva, Ohio, was made from a reduced version of *Hanover Tulip*, a pattern by Beverley Cosby of Mechanicsville, Virginia, for the Piecemakers Chapter of the Richmond Quilters' Guild; the pattern originally appeared in *Great American Quilts, 1992*, published by Oxmoor House, Birmingham, Alabama. Photographed by David Thum of Lakewood, Ohio (page 38).

Miniature Sunbonnet Sue (page 6) was appliquéd and quilted by Leita E. Shahan of Geneva, Ohio, in 1994 from a traditional design. Photographed by David Thum of Lakewood, Ohio.

Miniature Basket was appliquéd and quilted by Leita E. Shahan of Geneva, Ohio, in 1994 from a traditional design. Photographed by Larry London (page 40).

Birds of a Feather was designed, appliquéd, and quilted by Fran Soika of Novelty, Ohio. Photographed by Larry London (page 35).

Images of Spain was designed, appliquéd, and quilted by Fran Soika in 1993. Photographed by Larry London (page 41).

Mimbres Turtles was designed, appliquéd, and quilted by Fran Soika of Novelty, Ohio. Photographed by Larry London (page 30).

Acoma was designed, appliquéd, and quilted by Fran Soika of Novelty, Ohio in 1988 from patterns based on traditional Acoma Indian pottery designs by Drew (Andrew H.) Lewis of San Fidel, New Mexico. Photographed by Larry London (page 38).

Urban Garden was designed, appliquéd, and quilted by Judith Kessler Smith of Euclid, Ohio, in 1993. Photographed by Larry London (page 39).

Homage to Georgia O'Keeffe II and III were designed, appliquéd, and quilted by Nancy L. Watts of Rocky River, Ohio, in 1993. Photographed by David Thum of Lakewood, Ohio (pages 32 and 33).

I Remember Santa Skating on Mistletoe Pond was appliquéd and quilted by Edith Trocchio of Canton, Ohio from a pattern by De Selby, formerly of Hickory Hollow, Versailles, Kentucky, now residing in South Glamorgan, Wales. Photographed by Larry London (page 44).

Pattern block photos, pages 45–62, by Jack Ward, Inc., New York.

Metric Equivalents

Inches	MM	CM	Inches	CM	Inches	CM
1/8	3	0.3	9	22.9	30	76.2
1/4	6	0.6	10	25.4	31	78.7
3/8	10	1.0	11	27.9	32	81.3
1/2	13	1.3	12	30.5	33	83.8
5/8	16	1.6	13	33.0	34	86.4
3/4	19	1.9	14	35.6	35	88.9
7/8	22	2.2	15	38.1	36	91.4
1	25	2.5	16	40.6	37	94.0
1 1/4	32	3.2	17	43.2	38	96.5
1 1/2	38	3.8	18	45.7	39	99.1
1 3/4	44	4.4	19	48.3	40	101.6
2	51	5.1	20	50.8	41	104.1
2 1/2	64	6.4	21	53.3	42	106.7
3	76	7.6	22	55.9	43	109.2
3 1/2	89	8.9	23	58.4	44	111.8
4	102	10.2	24	61.0	45	114.3
4 1/2	114	11.4	25	63.5	46	116.8
5	127	12.7	26	66.0	47	119.4
6	152	15.2	27	68.6	48	121.9
7	178	17.8	28	71.1	49	124.5
8	203	20.3	29	73.7	50	127.0

MM—millimetres   CM—centimetres

Index